Is For Aboriginal

This book is dedicated to my parents

Joe and Virginia (née Doyle) MacLean

for the love and respect that they instilled in me
for language and education.

Author's Palindrome: No evil I did, I live on.

Acknowledgements

I acknowledge that this book was written in the traditional territory of the
Coast Salish people.

I would like to thank my friends, colleagues and co-workers in the Aboriginal community
for the many opportunities that I have been given to understand the diverse and rich fabric
of Aboriginal history, art and culture.

I would like to recognize the excellent work done by Shawn Robertson on the research
and compilation of the glossary. Thank you Shawn - couldn't have done it without you.

I want to thank my friend, Sharon Lisette, for proofing this reader. We really needed
a pair of fresh eyes at the end of a long journey and the obvious (and not so obvious)
mistakes that she found would have been 'glaring' had she not lent a hand.

My most special thanks and appreciation goes out to my friend and collaborator,
Brendan Heard (the illustrator of this reader). His artful and understanding translation
of these simple thought poems into works of art has given this book a life unto itself.
Thank you Brendan.

Is For Aboriginal

First Nations Reader Series

written by joseph maclean
illustrated by brendan heard

© 2013

Interactive Publishing Corporation

North Vancouver, BC

Canada

www.aisforaboriginal.com

info@aisforaboriginal.com

Is For Aboriginal

The First People

Ten Thousand Years?
A hundred Thousand?

The first People on this land

Across the ice bridge?
By Canoe?
On the Turtle's back?

Some are gone
We are here to stay

Aboriginal
The First Nations

A'ananin, Abenaki, Acadia, Accohannock, Achumawi, Acjachemem, Acolhua, Acoma, Adai, Ahousaht, Ahtna, Ainu, Aitchelitz, Akha, Akimel O'odham, Akokisa, Akwesasne, Akwa'ala, Alabama-Coushatta, Alacalufe, Aleut, Algonquin, Alliklik, Alnôbak, Alsea, Alutiiq, Anasazi, Andaste, Ani-Stohini/Unami, Ani-Tsalagi, Anishinaabeg (Anishnaabe), Aniyunwiya, Antoniaño, Apache, Apalachee, Apalachicola, Applegate, Apsáalooke, Apwaruge, Arapaho, Araucano, Arawak, Arikara, Asháninka, Ashcroft Indian Band, Assateagues, Assiniboine, Atakapa, Atchatchakangouen, Atfalati, Athabascan, Atikamekw, Atsina, Atsugewi, Attawandaron, Avoyel, Ayisiyiniwok, Aymara, Aztec

Is For Beothuk

These people are gone

The Beothuk are no more

Remember Nancy Shanawdithit

The Beothuk met the first white men
The Vikings

Columbus did not discover America

Red ochre coloured their skin
Red skin

Babine, Bannock, Bantu, Barbareño, Bari, Barona, Basque, Báxoje, Bear River,

Beaver, Becher Bay, Bella Bella, Bella Coola, Beothuks (Betoukuag), Berber, Bidai,

Biloxi, Bisaya, Black Carib, Blackfoot (Blackfeet), Blood Tribe, Blueberry River,

BOḰEĆEN, Bora, Bribri, Brulè, Buryat

Is For Canoe

From the Arawak 'Canoa'
A Native Caribbean word
Ten thousand years of trade
Over a continent, along the coasts
and across the seas

The Great Western Red Cedar
Sixty man dugouts paddling to Hawaii
Light and agile birch bark vessels
plying the river ways both great and small
Bone and hide
kayaking the arctic floes

Caddo, Cahita, Cahto, Cahuilla, Calapooya, Calusa (Caloosa), Carcross/Tagish, Carib, Carquin, Carrier, Catawba, Cayuga, Cayuse, Chahta, Chappaquiddick, Chawathil, Cheam, Chehalis, Chelan, Chemainus, Chemehuevi, Cheraw, Cheroenhaka, Cherokee, Cheslatta Carrier Nation, Chetco, Cheyenne, Chickamauga, Chickasaw, Chicora, Chilcotin, Chilula, Chimariko, Chinook, Chippewa, Chipewyan, Chiricahua, Chitimacha, Choctaw, Choinumni, Chontal, Chowchila (Chawchila), Chukchansi, Chumash, Clackamas, Clatskanie, Clatsop-Nehalem, Cochimí, Cochiti, Cocopa, Coeur d'Alene, Cofan, Coharie, Columbia, Colville, Comanche, Comcaac, Comox, Conestogga, Confederated Tribes of Coos, Siuslaw and Lower Umpqua, Conoy, Constance Lake First Nation, Coos (Coosan), Coldwater, Copper River Athabascan, Coquille, Cora, Coso, Costanoan, Coushatta, Cowichan, Cowlitz, Cree, Creek, Croatan, Crow, Cuna, Cucupa, Cuncos, Cupeño (Cupa), Cup'ik

Is For Deganawidah

Prophet leader peacemaker

The great tree of peace

Father of the
Haudenosaunee (Iroquois)
Confederacy

Five Nations - then Six

The inspiration for the American
Constitution

Dakelh, Dakota, Dakubetede, Da̱'naxda̱'xw/A̱waetla̱la̱, Danezaa,

Deg Xinag (Deg Hit'an), Delaware, Dena'ina (Denaina), Dene, Dene Tha',

Diegueño, Dine (Dineh), Ditidaht First Nation, Dogon, Dogrib, Dumna,

Duwamish (DKhw'Duw'Absh), Dzawada̱'enux̱w

Is For Elder

A very special name

A very special place in
Aboriginal culture

Holders of Tradition

Listen and Learn
from the Elders
The living connection
to the past

Eansketambawg, Echota, Edisto, Eel River, Eenou (Eeyou), Embera-Wounaan,

Erie, Esk'etemc, Esselen, Esquimalt, Etchemin (Etchimin), Euchee, Eudeve (Endeve),

Evenks, Eyak

Is For First Nations

The Indigenous People
First Nations First People
Mètis and Inuit

Native Americans   Aborigines
San   Pygmies   Hill Tribes
the Adivasi or Scheduled Tribes

Many many names in many many lands

5000 peoples
350 million stories

Oh, to speak with one voice
would we not hear the heart

Fernandeño /Tatavian, Flathead Salish, Fond du Lac,

Fort Nelson First Nation, Fox

Is For Great Spirit

The Great Mystery
The Creator
Wakan Tanka   Gitchi Manitou

Maheo, Olelbis, Isakakate, Maxematasooma,
Maheo, Raweno, Yuttore Ixtcibenihehat,

Ababinili, Agu'gux, Caddi Ayo, Coyote,
Kitanitowit, Kisulkw Nishanu, Nitosi, Napi, Spi-
der Grandmother, Gici Niwaskw, Unetlanvhi,
Weshemoneto

Great Spirit has many names
The Creator speaks to each of
us in our own tongue

Gabrielino (Gabrieleño), Gaigwu, Galibi, Garifuna, Gashowu, Gila River, Gitga'at,

Gitxaala, Gitxsan (Gitksan), Goshute, Grand Ronde, Gros Ventre, Guarani,

Guarijio (Guarijío), Gwich'in (Gwitchin)

H

Is For Hiawatha

The Peacemaker's statesman
The great chief sought peace and
helped build the League
of Peace and Power
His oratory ended the warring
One arrow will easily break
hold many and they cannot be broken
The hatchets were buried and
the white tree of peace was planted

An American Constitution
on Turtle Island
before the Magna Carta
The Haudenosaunee Confederacy

Hadzabe, Haida, Haisla, Halfway River, Hän, Hanis, Hare, Haudenosaunee,
Hasinai, Havasupai, Hawaiian, Heiltsuk, Heve, Hiaki, Hitchiti, Hidatsa, Hmong,
Ho-Chunk, Hohe, Holikachuk, Homalco, Hoopa, Hopi, Hopland Pomo, Houma,
Hualapai, Huaorani, Huelel, Huichol, Huilliche, Hunkpapa, Hupa,
Hupacasath, Huron, Huu-ay-aht

Is For Indian

An Italian
Working for the Spanish
Seeking the Spice Islands
got lost

Thought he found the sea route
to India
Indian — a name to be forgotten

a name to be remembered

Illini (Illiniwek, Illinois), Inca, Inde, Ineseño (Inezeño), Ingalik (Ingalit), Innoko,

Innu, In-SHUCK-ch, Inuit, Inupiat (Inupiaq, Inupiatun),

Iowa-Oto (Ioway), Iroquois, Ishak, Isleño,

Itza Maya (Itzah), Iviatim

J

Is For Juniper

A sacred tree

ancient Druids

Buddist and Shamans

Europe and Asia

from the earth, all over the earth

Juniper is sacred

Jackson Rancheria Band, Jamestown S'Klallam, Jamul, Jena Band,

Jemez Pueblo, Jicarilla Apache, Juaneño

Is For Kanata

The Huron-Iroquois word for village or settlement

In 1535 Jacques Cartier met two youths who pointed to the Stadacona settlement

Now, Quebec City and the name for Canada

We live in a village

Kanata - Canada

Kadohadacho, Kainai, Kalapuya, Kali'na, Kalispel, Kanak, Kanaka Maoli, Kanien'kehá:ka, Kanza, Karankawa, Karen, Karkin, Karuk, Kashaya, Kaska Dena, Kaskaskia, Kathlamet, Kato, Katzie, Kaw, Kawaiisu, Kawèsqar, Kawlic, Kenaitze, Kewa Pueblo, Kichai, Kickapoo, Kilatikas, Kiliwa, Kiowa Apache, Kispiox/Anspayaxw, Kitanemuk, Kitasoo/Xai'xais, Kitselas, Kizh, Klahoose, Klallam, Klamath, Klickitat, Kogi, K'ómoks, Koorie, Kootenai, Korowai, Korubo, Koso, Koyukon, Ktunaxa, Kumeyaay, Kuna, Kwakiutl, Kwakwaka'wakw, Kwanlin Dün, Kwantlen, Kwiakah, Kwicksutaineuk-ah-kwa-mish

L

Is For Land

A sacred trust

Ten thousand years of bounty

Not for a few years of profit

The people are of the earth

We remember We protect

Steward the earth for the young
ones yet to come

Laguna, Lahu, Lake Babine Nation, Lakota, Lassik, Lawa,

Lax Kw'alaams, Lemhi Shoshone, Lenape (Lenni-Lenape), Lenca, Lil'wat,

Lipan Apache, Listiguj (Listuguj), Lisu, Lnuk (L'nuk, L'nu'k, Lnu), Lokono,

Loucheux (Loucheaux), Loup, Lower Chehalis, Lower Coquille, Lower Cowlitz,

Lower Umpqua, Lubicon, Luckiamute, Luiseño, Lumbee, Lummi, Lytton

Is For Mother

You have a mother
I have a mother
The earth is our mother
All living things are born of their
mother
The love of a mother can hold back
the
storm
Remember the mothers

Maasai, Macushi, Mahican, Maidu, Makah, Malahat, MÁLEXEŁ, Maliseet, Mandan,

Manobo, Maori, Mapuche, Maricopa, Massachusett, Massasoit, Matawa,

Matlatzinca, Mattabesset, Mattaponi, Mattole, Maumee, Maya, Mayo,

Mdewkanton, Mechoopda, Mengwe, Menominee (Menomini), Meskwaki (Mesquakie),

Mètis, Metlakatla, Miami-Illinois, Miccosukee, Mi'kmaq, Migueleño, Mingo, Miniconjou,

Minqua, Minsi, Miskitu, Missouria, Mississauga, Mississinewas, Mississipian,

Miwok (Miwuk), Mixe, Mixtec (Mixteco, Mixteca), Mlabri, Modoc, Mohave, Mohawk,

Mohegan, Mohican, Mojave, Molala, Monacan, Monache (Mono), Mosopelea,

Montaukett, Mosopelea, Multnomah, Munsee, Muskogee, Musqueam

N

Is For Native

Native Plant
Native Land
Native People
Native Son
Native tongue

Hold to your roots for they reach far beyond time

Nadot'en, Nadouessioux, Naga, Nahane (Nahani, Nahanne), Nahua,
Nakoda (Nakota), 'Namgis, Nambe Pueblo, Nanticoke, Nantucket, Narragansett,
Naskapi, Natchez, Navajo (Navaho), Nawat, Nde, Nee-me-poo (Nimiipuu, Nimi'ipu),
Nehiyaw (Nehiyawok), Nentego, Neusiok, Neutrals, Newe, Nez Perce, Ngarrindjeri,
Niantic, Nicola, Nipmuc, Nisga'a, Nisenan (Nishinam), Nishnawbe Aski, Niitsitapi,
Nlaka'pamux (Nlakapamux), Nomlaki, Nootka (Nutka), Nootsack,
Northern Cheyenne, Northern Tutchone, Nottoway, Nunga,
Nuu-chah-nulth, Nuwu, Nuxalk, Nyoongar

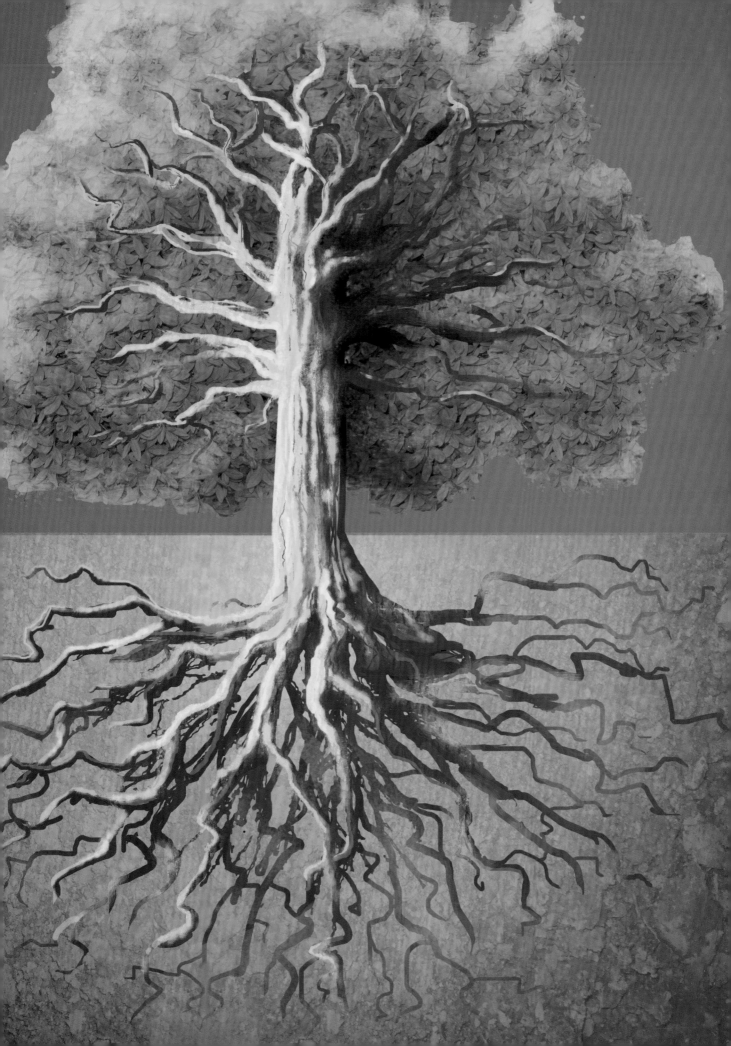

Is For Origin

Look to the names
Look to the foods
Look to the places
We say
We eat
We live

in a world of original names — native
names - Aboriginal names

Canada, canoe, tobacco, hurricane,
chocolate, hammock, tomato

Can you find more?

Odawa, Ofo, Oglala, Ogoni, Ohkay Owingeh, Ohlone, Ojibwe (Ojibway, Ojibwa),

Oji-Cree, Okanagan (Okanogan), Okwanuchu, Omaha, Oneida, Onondaga,

O'odham (Oodham), Opata, Osage, Osoyoos, Otoe (Oto),

Otoe-Missouria, Ottawa, Ouiatenon

P Is For Potlach

Wealth is giving
The Potlatch
The once outlawed
economy of the Pacific Northwest
Greatness and power, measured by the
ability to give and share
A hopeful model for the future
A better economy - a better world
The greatness of sharing

Like the constitution it was already here
but not adopted
Time is long
The future is in sharing

Pacheedaht First Nation, Paipai, Paiute, Palus (Palouse), Pamlico, Panamint,
Pangasinan, Pascua Yaqui, Passamaquoddy, Patuxet, Patwin,
Paugussett (Paugusset), Pauquachin, Pawnee,
Pechanga Band of Luiseno Mission Indians, Pee Dee, Pehuenche, Pend D'Oreilles,
Penobscot (Pentagoet), Peoria, Pequot, Piankeshaw, Picuris, Piegan (Piikani), Pima,
Pipil, Piscataway, Pit River, Pocomoke, Pocumtuck, Pojoaque, Pomo (Pomoan),
Ponca, Popoluca (Popoloca), Potawatomi (Pottawatomie), Powhatan,
Pueblo, Putún, Puyallup

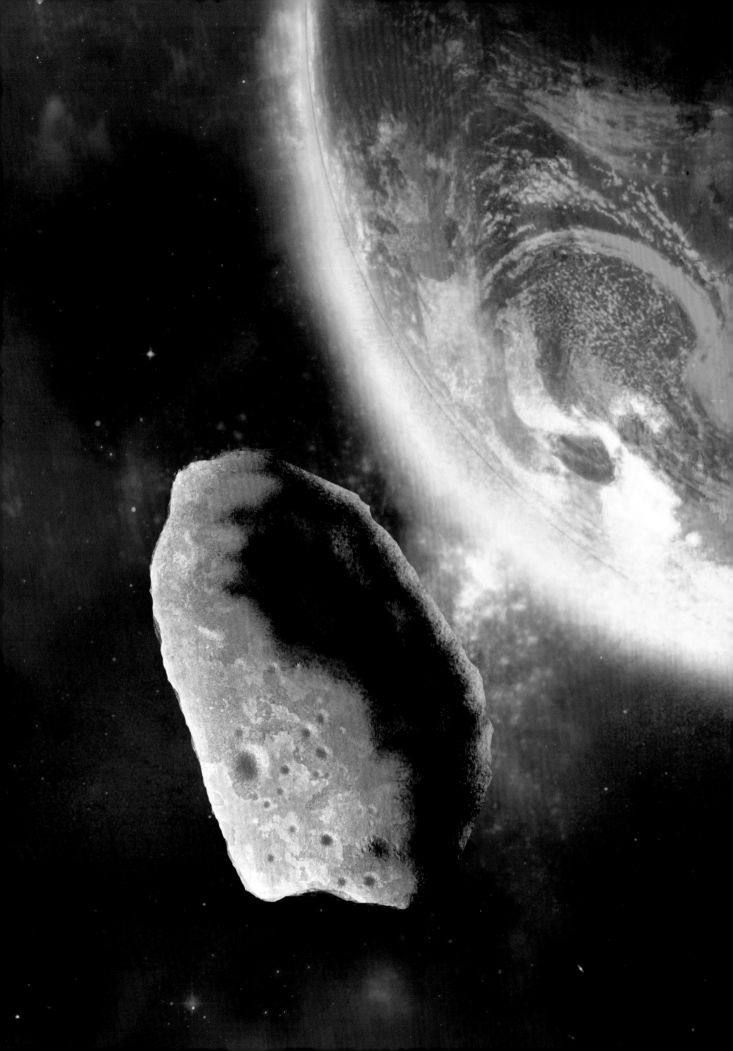

Is For Question

Who am I?

Who are we?

Where do we come from?
From a Nation
From a State
From our mother
From the earth

Original and unique
Celebrate, rejoice and

Be who you are

Q'anjob'al, Qualicum, Quapaw (Quapa), Quasmigdo, Qayqayt, Quechan, Quechua,
Quilcene, Quileute, Quinault, Quinnipiac (Quinnipiack), Quiripi

Is For Reservation

Reserve judgement
Preserve heritage
Residential schools hurt the people
It is the solemn reserve of the elders
that carries the generations forward

Sadness, yes
Pain, Yes

The test of time is
in the heart of those
that remember and persevere
for those that will come after

A happy heritage is one that sees the
children dance

Raramuri, Restigouche, Roanoke, Rumsen

S

Is For Sasquatch

Wandering the woods
high in the mountains
The myth pervades
North America, Asia and beyond
The Yeti
The Abominable Snowman
Mythical creatures abound in many
cultures
Have you seen the Sasquatch?

Saanich, Sac, Sahaptin, Sahtu, Saik'uz, Salhulhtxw, Salinan, Salish, Sami, Samish, Sammamish, San, Sandia, San Felipe Pueblo, San Ildefonso Pueblo, Sanish (Sahnish), San Juan Southern Paiute Tribe, Sanpoil, Santa Ana Pueblo, Santa Clara Pueblo, Santee, Santiam, Santo Domingo Pueblo, Saponi, Sarcee (Sarsi), Sastean (Sasta), Satsop, Sauk, Sauk-Suiattle, Saulteaux, Savannah, Schaghticoke (Scaticook), Scia'new, Scw'exmx, Sechelt, Secwepemc (Secwepmectsin), Sekani, Selkirk, Seminole, SEMYOME (Semiahmoo), Seneca, Seri, Serrano, Severn Ojibwe, Shanel, Shasta (Shastan), Shawnee, Shinnecock, Shipibo, Shoshone, Shuar, Shuswap, Siksika (Siksikáwa), Siletz, Similkameen, Sinkiuse, Sinkyone, Sioux, Sisseton Wahpeton, Siuslaw, Skagit, Skicin, S'Klallam, Skokomish, Skraeling, Slavey (Slave, Slavi), Sliammon (Sliamon), Sm'algyax, Snake, Snohomish, Snoqualmie, Snuneymuxw, Songhees, Songish, Sooke, Souriquois (Sourquois), Southern Paiute, Southern Tutchone, Spaxomin, Spokane (Spokan), Squaxin, Skwxwú7mesh (Squamish), St'at'imc (Stl'atl'imx), Stillaquamish, Stockbridge-Munsee, Sto:lo, Stoney, Sts'ailes, Stswecem'c Xgat'tem, Stz'uminus, Sugpiaq, Sukuma, Suma, Susquehannock, Suquamish, Swampy Cree, Swinomish, SXIMEȽEȽ (Esquimalt), Syilx

Is For Totem

Odoodem
Ojibwe for clan

Elders and carvers have many names for poles
Welcome poles
Story Poles
Clan Poles
Door posts and others
Look at the poles
What do they say?
This is where the law was recorded

Tabasco Chontal, Tachi (Tache), Taensa, Tagish, Tahltan, Taidnapam, Taino,
Tainui, Takelma, Takla, Takudh, Taltushtuntede, Tamoucougoula, Tamyen,
Tanaina, Tanana, Tanêks(a), Tano, Taos Pueblo, Tarahumara, Taroko,
Tataviam, TÁ,UTW̱ (Tsawout), Tawakoni, Tawas, Tawira (Tauira), Tehachapi,
Ten'a, Tenino, Tepehuano (Tepecano), Tesuque, Tetawken, Tetes-de-Boules,
Tewa, Thompson, Tigua, Tillamook, Timbisha (Timbasha), Timucua, Tinde,
Tionontati, Tiwa, Tla A'min, Tla-o-qui-aht, Tlahuica (Tlahura), TZ̨įchǫ, Tlingit,
Toba, Tohono O'odham, Tolowa, Tongva, Tonkawa, Totonacs, Towa,
Tr'ondëk Hwëch'in, Tsalagi (Tsa-la-gi), Tsalagiyi Nvdagi, Tsartlip, Tsattine,
Tsawwassen, Tsetsaut, Tsetsehestahese, Tseycum, Tsilhqot'in, Tsimshian,
Ts'ishaa7ath (Tseshaht), Tsitsistas, Tsleil-Waututh, Tsnungwe, T'sou-ke,
Tsoyaha, Tsuu T'ina (Tsuutina), Tualatin, Tuareg, Tubatulabal, Tulalip,
Tumpisa (Tümbisha, Tumbisha), Tunica, Tupi, Tuscarora, Tutchone, Tutelo,
Tututni, Twana, Twatwa (Twightwee)

Is For Understanding

The flower is kissed by the bee
The plant grows food for the people
Nature thrives on difference
Dancing with the difference

Share the dance
Celebrate the difference
Understand that we are all the same

Be happy with your difference

Uchucklesaht, Ucluelet, Ukomnom, Unama'ki Mi'kmaq, Unangan (Unangax), Umatilla,

Unkechaug (Unquachog), Umpqua (Unquachog), Upper Chehalis,

Upper Cowlitz, Upper Nicola, Ute, U'wa, Uchee

Is For Values

Respect oneself and others

Preserve earth's bounty

Compassion for all of
the creator's creatures

Moderation in all things

Fairness in ones dealings

Honesty with oneself and
towards others

Virginian Algonkin, Vuntut Gwitchin

Is For Wigwam

Wigwam
Wickiup
Many styles Many Nations
many many places
One of the oldest

Have you seen a sweat lodge?
Our mothers and grandmothers are
remembered in the shape
A living tradition
Living on in this land

Wabanaki, Wahpekute, Wanapum, Wauzhushk Onigum, Wailaki (Wailakki),

Wailatpu (Waylatpu), Walapai, Walla Walla, Wampano, Wampanoag, Wappinger,

Wappo, Warm Springs, Wasco-Wishram, Washo (Washoe), Wazhazhe,

W̱CȈÁNEW̱ (Becher Bay), Wea, Wenatchi (Wenatchee), Wendat, Weott, Wenro,

Westbank, Wet'suwet'en, Whilkut, White Clay People, Wichita (Witchita), Wikchamni,

Wikwemikong, Willapa (Willopah), Winnebago, Wintu (Wintun), Wiradjuri, Wet'suwet'en,

WJOȽEȽP (Tsartlip), Wiyot (Wi'yot, Wishosk), Wolastoqewi (Wolastoqiyik), W̱SÁNEĆ,

W̱SÌKEM (Tseycum), Wuikinuxv, Wyandot (Wyandotte)

Is For Xa:ytem

The Fraser River Valley
The traditional Stó:lo territory

Ten thousand years
years beyond counting
years beyond memory
The Stó:lo remain

The legend of the transformer stone:
Three Siya:m (respected leaders)
failed in their duty to share their
knowledge and were 'suddenly
transformed' into stone

xa:ytem: sudden transformation

Xai'xais, Xavante, Xat'súll, Xaxli'p, Xa'xtsa, Xeni Gwet'in

Is For Yana

Yana and Ishi died together in 1916
Yana was Ishi's language
Ishi was the last Yana speaker
His language died with him.
Yana meant people
Ishi is the Yana word for man
Ishi told that he had
no name for there
was no one to name him

Two more languages - Yoncalla and
Yuki too have gone

Yana, Yakama, Yakuts, Yamasee, Yanesha, Yanomami, Yao, Yaqui, Yaquina,

Yavapai-Apache, Yazoo, Yekooche, Yinka Dene, Yocot'an, Yoeme, Yokaia (Yakaya),

Yokuts (Yokut, Yokutsan), Yolngu, Ysleta del Sur,

Yucatec Maya (Yucateco, Yucatan), Yuchi (Yuchee), Yuin,

Yuki (Yukian), Yuma, Yupik (Yu'pik, Yuit), Yurok (Yu'rok)

Z

Is For Zuni

Pueblo
From the Spanish for Village

Ancient Anasazi
American Southwest

A:shiwi is their name in their language
The language stands alone
unique, single, their own

Zuni pottery
geometry and rich secrets
glaze and gleam in the desert sun

Zapotec, Zia, Zimshian, Zuma (Zumana), Zoque, Zuni

A'ananin (See Gros Ventre)

Abenaki (also Alnôbak or Alnanbal)

The Abenaki (People of the Dawnlands) are one of the Algonquian-speaking peoples of northeastern North America. The Abenaki live in the New England region of the United States and Quebec and the Maritimes of Canada. The Abenaki are one of the five members of the Wabanaki Confederacy. They call themselves the Alnôbak or Alnanbal.

Acadia

Acadia First Nation is composed of five reserves spread throughout the South Western shore of Nova Scotia and across three counties.

Accohannock

The Accohannock are an Algonquian-speaking sub-Tribe of the Powhatan Nation. The bands of the Accohannock were part of the Accomac Confederation. They were the first watermen, hunters, farmers, and trappers on the Chesapeake Bay waters and wetlands.

Achumawi

The Achomawi (also Achumawi, Ajumawi and Ahjumawi) are one of eleven bands of the Pit River Tribe of Native Americans who lived in what is now North Eastern California in the United States.

Acjachemem

The Acagchemem or Juaneño are an indigenous Tribe of Southern California. The Juaneño lived in what is now part of Orange and San Diego Counties.

Acolhua

The Acolhua are a Mesoamerican people who arrived in the Valley of Mexico in or around the year 1200 CE. The Acolhua were a sister culture of the Aztecs (or Mexica) as well as the Tepanec, Chalca, Xochimilca and others.

Acoma

Acoma Pueblo is a Native American pueblo approximately sixty miles west of Albuquerque, New Mexico. One of the oldest continuously inhabited communities in the United States. Acoma tribal traditions estimate that they have lived in the village for more than two thousand years.

Adai

Adai (also Adaizan, Adaizi, Adaise, Adahi, Adaes, Adees, Atayos) is the name of a Native American people of North Western Louisiana and North Eastern Texas with a South Eastern culture. The name Adai is derived from the Caddo word hadai meaning "brushwood." The Adai were among the first peoples in North America to experience European contact—and were profoundly affected. In 1530 Álvar Núñez Cabeza de Vaca writes of them using the name Atayos. The Adai subsequently moved away from their homeland. By 1820, there were only thirty persons remaining. Their language is possibly Caddoan, but remains unclassified due to a lack of attestation.

Ahousaht

Ahousaht means people of Ahous, a small bay on the west side of Vargas Island in Clayoquot Sound. Ahousaht can be translated to mean 'people living with their backs to the land and mountains on a beach along the open sea.' Ahousaht First Nation territory encompasses much of Clayoquot Sound with the village of Maaqtusiis (Marktosis Indian Reserve IR #15) being the only reserve or village site inhabited year-round. Ahousaht First Nation has 25 reserve sites within the nation's territories, all accessible only by floatplane or boat. (Source: http://ahousaht.ca/Home.html)

Ahtna

The Ahtna (also Ahtena, Atna, Ahtna-kohtaene, or Copper River) are one of the Tribes of Athabaskan people in Alaska. The Tribe's homeland is located in the Copper River area of southern Alaska, and the name Ahtna derives from the local name for the Copper River. The name Ahtena, also written as Ahtna and Atnatana, translates as "ice people."

Ainu

The Ainu are indigenous people or groups in Japan and Russia. Historically, they spoke the Ainu language and related varieties and lived in Hokkaido, the Kuril Islands, and much of Sakhalin.

Aitchelitz First Nation

The Aitchelitz First Nation, also known as the Aitchelitz Band, is a First Nations band government of the Sto:lo people, located at Sardis, British Columbia, Canada (Chilliwack). It is a member of the Sto:lo Nation Tribal Council.

Akha

The Akha are an indigenous hill Tribe that live in small villages at high altitudes in the mountains of Thailand, Burma, Laos, China, and Yunnan Province in China. They made their way from China into South East Asia during the early 1900s. Civil war in Burma and Laos resulted in an increased flow of Akha immigrants and there are now some 80,000 living in Thailand's northern provinces of Chiang Rai and Chiang Mai where they constitute one of the largest of the hill Tribes.

Akimel O'odham (See Pima)

Akokisa

The Akokisa were the indigenous Tribe that lived on Galveston Bay and the lower Trinity and San Jacinto rivers in Texas, primarily in the present-day Greater Houston area. They are regarded as a band of the Atakapa, closely related to the Atakapa of Lake Charles, Louisiana.

Akwa'ala (See PaiPai)

Akwesasne

Akwesasne borders the countries of Canada and the United States of America; the Canadian Provinces of Ontario and Quebec; and the American State of New York. Despite the apparent difficulties of this multi-jurisdictional location, this Mohawk community of about 13,000 Peoples, has learned how to maneuver effectively, to make the best that we can of our situation. Despite the negative media coverage concerning the use of some of our People in unrestrained cross-border enterprise, our People have been able to create an honorable, and viable Mohawk society and an strong economic base for its People. (Source: http://akwesasne.ca/history.html)

Alabama-Coushatta

The Alabama or Alibamu (Albaamaha in the Alabama language) are a Southeastern indigenous Native American group, originally from Mississippi. They were members of the Muscogee Creek Confederacy, a loose trade and military organization of autonomous towns; their homelands were on the upper Alabama River. The Alabama and closely allied Coushatta migrated from Alabama and Mississippi to the area of Texas in the late 18th century and early 19th century under pressure from European-American settlers to the east. They essentially merged and shared reservation land.

Alacalufe

The Alacaluf (also Halakwulup, Kawésqar, or Kaweskar) are a South American people living in the Chilean Patagonia, specifically in the Brunswick Peninsula, and Wellington, Santa Inés, and Desolación islands. Their traditional language is known as Kawésqar. They were a nomadic seafaring people until the twentieth century. Because of their maritime culture, the Kawésqar have never farmed the land.

Aleut

Aleut people are the indigenous people of the Aleutian Islands of Alaska and Kamchatka Krai, Russia. The name "Aleut" comes from the Aleut word allíthuh, meaning "community." A regional self-denomination is Unangax◉, Unangan or Unanga, meaning "original people."

Algonquin

The Algonquin (also known as the Algonkin) were a small Tribe that lived in northern Michigan and Canada (specifically Southern Quebec and Eastern Ontario). Many confuse the term "Algonquin" with "Algonquian", which refers to a large number of Native American languages. The Algonquin Tribe is just one of the many Algonquian

-speaking Tribes in North America. They originally lived in the present-day United States, but were forced away from their homeland when the Iroquois League formed and took over the area.

Alliklik

A Shoshonean people in the upper Santa Clara river valley, California. "The Alliklik Indians led Don Gaspar de Portola over the pass in 1767 and this is believed to be when the first white man entered the valley. The Allikliks lived in four rancherias; the largest was near Castaic Junction. Their homes were reed huts, clustered in groups of eight or ten, making up a village of 25 or so people. There were probably no more than five hundred Allikliks alive at any one time since their arrival here in 500 AD. The last of this proud race vanished from the face of the earth before 1920.(Source: californiadar.org/chapters/alliklik/alliklikhistory2001.htm)

Alnôbak

The Alnôbak Wabanakiak (also Alnombak) inhabited the land they called Ndakinna. This group included the Western Abenaki, who inhabited the land that today includes all of Vermont, New Hampshire, north-central Massachusetts, northwestern Maine, and southern Quebec. It is estimated that before contact with Europeans, the Western Abenaki population in Vermont was 10,000.

Alsea

The Alsea (Älsé, Alseya) were a Native American Tribe of Western Oregon. They are probably extinct, although a few members may be mixed in with the Confederated Tribes of Siletz many live on the Siletz Reservation where the remaining members were relocated.

Alutiiq

The Alutiiq are a southern coastal people of the Native peoples of Alaska. Their language is called Sugstun. They are not to be confused with the Aleuts, who live further to the southwest, including along the Aleutian Islands.

Anasazi

The Ancient Puebloans (Anasazi) were a prehistoric Native American civilization centered around the present day Four Corners area of the Southwest United States. They are collectively considered the ancestors of the modern Pueblo peoples, including the Hopi, Zuni and the Puebloans. The word "Anasazi is Navajo for "Ancient Ones" or "Ancient Enemy."

Andaste (Also see Susquehannock)

Andaste (Andastes in plural) is the French name for the Susquehannock people. The name is derived from the Huron, another Iroquoian-speaking people, who called these people Andastoerrhonon, meaning "people of the blackened ridge pole", this was related to their building practices.

Anishinaabeg (Anishinaabe)

Anishinaabeg or Anishinabek,(more commonly; Anishinaabe or Anishinabe), is the autonym often used by the Odawa, Ojibwe, and Algonquin peoples. They all speak closely related Anishinaabemowin/Anishinaabe languages, of the Algonquian language family. The meaning of Anishnaabeg is 'First' or 'Original Peoples'.

Ani-Stohini/Unami

Ani-Stohini/Unami is a small Native American Tribe located in seven counties of the Blue Ridge Mountains of Virginia and one county of North Carolina. The Tribe, historically part of the Algonquian-language family, was one of the major branches of the Delaware Tribe.

Ani-Tsalagi (See Tsalagiyi Nvdagi)

Aniyunwiya (Also see Cherokee)

Aniyunwiya (also: Keetoowah, Tsalagi) is the original name that the Cherokee called themselves. The name Cherokee is derived from the Creek word for the Aniyunwiya. Sequoyah (c. 1770–1840), named in English George Gist or George Guess, was a Cherokee silversmith. In 1821 he completed his independent creation of a Cherokee syllabary, making reading and writing in Cherokee possible. This was the only time in recorded history that a member of a non-literate people independently created an effective writing system. After seeing its worth, the people of the Cherokee Nation rapidly began to use his syllabary and officially adopted it in 1825. Their literacy rate quickly surpassed that of surrounding European-American settlers.

Antoniaño (See Salinan)

Apache (See Tinde)

Apalachee

The Apalachee were a Native American people who historically lived in the Florida Panhandle. The Apalachee occupied the site of Velda Mound starting about 1450 CE, but had mostly abandoned it before the Spanish started settlements in the 17th century. They first encountered Spanish explorers in the 16th century, when the Hernando de Soto expedition arrived. They spoke a Muskogean language called Apalachee now extinct. Traditional tribal enemies, European diseases, and European encroachment severely reduced their population. The survivors dispersed, and over time many Apalachee integrated with other groups, particularly the Creek Confederacy, while others relocated to other Spanish territories, and some remained in what is now Louisiana. About 300 descendants in Rapides Parish, Louisiana, assert an Apalachee identity today.

Apalachicola

The Apalachicola, also called Pallachacola, were a group of Native Americans related to the Muscogee people. They spoke a Muskogean language related to Hitchiti. They lived along the Apalachicola River in present-day Florida. Their name probably derives from Hitchiti Apalachicoli or Muskogee Apalachicolo, signifying apparently "People of the other side," with reference probably to the Apalachicola River or some nearby stream.

Applegate (See Dakubetede)

Apsáalooke (Crow)

The Apsáalooke in their own Siouan language are more commonly known as the Crow. They historically lived in the Yellowstone River valley from Wyoming to North Dakota. Pressured by the Ojibwas and Cree, who had earlier and better access to guns through the fur trade, they had migrated there from Ohio to settle south of Lake Winnipeg, Canada. From there, they were pushed to the west by the Cheyennes. Both the Crow and the Cheyennes were then pushed further west by the Lakota (Sioux).

Apwaruge (See Atsugewi)

Arapaho

The Arapaho are a Tribe of Native Americans historically living on the eastern plains of Colorado and Wyoming. Arapaho is an Algonquian language. The Northern Arapaho Nation live on the Wind River Reservation in Wyoming and the Southern Arapaho Tribe live with the Southern Cheyenne in Oklahoma. Together their members are enrolled as a federally recognized tribe, the Cheyenne and Arapaho Tribes.

Araucano (See Mapuche)

Arawak

The Arawak people (from aru, the Lucayan word for cassava flour) are some of the indigenous peoples of the West Indies. The group belongs to the Arawakan language family. They were the indigenous people that Christopher Columbus encountered when he first arrived in the Americas in 1492.

Arikara

Arikara (Sanish, Sahnish), a Native American Tribe presently found in North Dakota forming the northern group of the Caddoan linguistic family. In language they differ only dialectically from the Pawnee.

Asháninka

The Asháninka or Asháninca are an indigenous people living in the rainforests of Peru and in the State of Acre Brazil.

Ashcroft First Nation

Ashcroft Indian Band is a First Nation community located in the Thompson Nicola Regional District of British Columbia. Our neighbouring communities are the Villages of Ashcroft to the west and Cache Creek in the south. We are part of the rich Nl'Akapxm Nation. (Source: http://ashcroftband.ca/)

Assateagues

The Assateagues or Assateague Indian Tribe are an Algonquian tribe speaking the Nanticoke language who historically lived on the Atlantic coast side of the Delmarva Peninsula (known during the colonial period as the Eastern Shores of Maryland and Virginia, and the Lower Counties of Pennsylvania). The Aboriginal Assateague chiefdom was adapted to the maritime and forest resources of the Chincoteague Bay watershed and involved in the manufacture and trade of shell beads.

Assiniboine (See Nakoda)

Atakapa

The Atakapa people are an indigenous people of the Southeastern Woodlands, who spoke the Atakapa language (extinct) and historically lived along the Gulf of Mexico. They called themselves the Ishak, pronounced "ee-SHAK", which translates as "The People" and further designated themselves within the Tribe as "The Sunrise People" and "The Sunset People." Although the people were decimated by infectious disease after European contact, descendants still live in Louisiana and Texas. Atakapa-Ishak descendants had a gathering in 2006.

Atchatchakangouen

In the 17th Century the Atchatchakangouen along with the Kilatika, Mengakonkia, Pepicokia, Wea, and Piankashaw came together and formed the Miami (Crane Band) The Pepicokia Tribe was brought into the Wea and Piankashaw Tribes, which when combined with the Miami proper formed the Miami Nation. (Source: geo.msu.edu/geogmich/Miamis.html)

Atfalati

The Atfalati, also known as the Tualatin were a tribe or band of the Kalapuya Native Americans who originally inhabited the Tualatin Valley in the northwest part of the U.S. state of Oregon. The Tribe had permanent villages they inhabited during the winter months located on the shores and vicinity of Wapato Lake and near Beaverton, Forest Grove, Gaston, and Hillsboro.

Athabascan

Athabaskan or Athabascan (also Den'a (Dene), Athapascan, Athapaskan) is a large group of indigenous peoples of North America, located in two main Southern and Northern groups in western North America. The Athabaskan language family is the second largest family in North America in terms of number of languages and the number of speakers.

Atikamekw

The Atikamekw are the indigenous inhabitants of the area they refer to as Nitaskinan ("Our Land"), in the upper Saint-Maurice River valley of Quebec. They have a tradition of agriculture as well as fishing, hunting and gathering. They have close traditional ties with the Innu people. The Atikamekw language, a variant of the Cree language in the Algonquian family, is still in everyday use.

Atsina (See Gros Ventre)

Atsugewi

The Atsugewi, are Native Americans residing in northeastern California, United States. Their traditional lands are near Mount Shasta, specifically the Pit River drainage on Burney, Hat, and Dixie Valley or Horse Creeks. They are closely related to the Achomawi and consisted of two groups (the Atsugé and the Apwaruge). The Atsugé ("pine-tree people") traditionally are from the Hat Creek area, and the Apwaruge ("juniper-tree people") are from the Dixie Valley. They lived to the south of the Achomawi.

Attawandaron

The Attawandaron, called Neutrals by the French, were an Iroquoian nation of North American indigenous people who lived near the northern shores of Lake Ontario and Lake Erie. During the late sixteenth and early seventeenth centuries, the territory of the Attawandaron was mostly within the limits of present-day southern Ontario. There was a single population cluster to the east, across the Niagara River near modern-day Buffalo, New York.

Avoyel (See Tamoucougoula)

Ayisiyiniwok (See Cree)

Aymara

The Aymara or Aimara are an indigenous ethnic group in the Andes and Altiplano regions of South America; about 2 million live in Bolivia, Peru and Chile. They lived in the region for many centuries before becoming a subject people of the Inca, and later of the Spanish in the 16th century. With the Spanish American Wars of Independence (1810-1825), Aymaras became subjects of Bolivia and Peru and after the War of the Pacific (1879-1883), Chile acquired the Aymaran population.

Aztec

The Aztecs were the Native American people who dominated northern Mexico at the time of the Spanish conquest in the early 16th century. A nomadic culture, the Aztecs eventually settled on several small islands in Lake Texcoco where, in 1325, they founded the town of Tenochtitlan, modern-day Mexico City. Fearless warriors and pragmatic builders, the Aztecs created an empire during the 15th century that was surpassed in size in the Americas only by that of the Incas in Peru. (Source: aztec.com)

Babine (See Lake Babine Nation)

Bannock

The Bannock Tribe of the Northern Paiute are an indigenous people of the Great Basin. Their traditional lands include southeastern Oregon, southeastern Idaho, western Wyoming and southwestern Montana. Today they are enrolled in the federally recognized Shoshone-Bannock Tribes of the Fort Hall Reservation of Idaho, located on the Fort Hall Indian Reservation.

Bantu

Bantu is used as a general label for 300-600 ethnic groups in Africa who speak Bantu languages, distributed from Cameroon east across Central Africa and Eastern Africa to Southern Africa. There are about 250 Bantu languages. The Bantu family is fragmented into hundreds of individual groups, none of them larger than a few million people (the largest being the Zulu with some 10 million). The Bantu language Swahili with its 5-10 million native speakers is of super-regional importance as tens of millions fluently command it as a second language.

Barbareño

The Barbareño Chumash Council is a tribal organization representing Chumash descendents whose ancestral villages were located in what is now the general Santa Barbara area. The Council is active in bringing Chumash people back to their maritime culture and revitalizing the Barbareño Chumash language. (Source: barbareno-chumashcouncil.com)

Bari

The Bari ethnic groups in South Sudan occupy the Savanna lands of the White Nile Valley. They speak a language that is also called Bari. The name "Bari of the Nile Valley" would be fitting because the river Nile runs through the heart of the Bari land.

Barona

In 1875, the federal government established the Capitan Grande Reservation for the people (Kumeyaay, Lipay and Diegueño) living in the area at that time. About 40 years later in 1932, the city literally bought the Capitan Grande Reservation to build a reservoir and the people were removed from their land. In 1932, without a homeland but with some federal monies allotted from the sale, a group of the Capitan Grande tribal members purchased the Barona Ranch which today is the Barona Indian Reservation near Lakeside, about 30 miles northeast of San Diego. (Source: barona-nsn.gov)

Basque

The origin of the Basque people has been shrouded in mystery. The Basques have occupied much the same area of northern Spain and southern France for thousands of years, extending further eastward and northwards into Gascony, and speak a language whose ties to other living languages are unclear at best. Nowadays it is accepted that most likely, the Basques are the last surviving people from a time of European prehistory when Indo-European languages were not yet widely spoken on the continent.

Báxoje (See Iowa-Oto)

Bear River First Nation

Bear River First Nation (also known as the L'sitkuk)is one of thirteen First Nation communities in Nova Scotia .... a proud member of the Confederacy of Mainland Mi'kmaq, a Tribal Council that provides advisory services and programs to member communities. Archeological evidence suggests that there has been continuous settlement by the L'sitkuk in the area for 3,000 to 4,000 years.

Beaver (See Dunne-za)

Becher Bay (Also Beecher Bay and now called the Scia'new (Cheauth) First Nation) (See WSÁNEĆ)

Bella Bella (See Heiltsuk)

Bella Coola (See Nuxalk)

Beothuk

The Beothuk (also spelled Beothic, Beothick, Beothuck and Betoukuag) were one of the historical Aboriginal peoples in Canada. The small group of people lived in present day Newfoundland at the time of European contact in the 15th and 16th centuries. With the 1829 death of Nancy Shanawdithit, a woman in her late twenties who was the last known living Beothuk, the people became officially extinct with her passing.

Berber

Berbers are the indigenous ethnic group of North Africa, west of the Nile Valley. A Berber person is not necessarily only someone who happens to speak Berber. The Berber identity is usually wider than language and ethnicity, and encompasses the entire history and geography of North Africa. Linguistically speaking, there are some 25 to 35 million Berber-language speakers in North Africa.

Bidai

The Bidai were a band of Atakapa Indians from eastern Texas. Their oral history says that the Bidai were the original peoples in their region. Their central settlements were along Bedias Creek, but their territory ranged from the Brazos River to the Neches River. Their name could be Caddo, meaning "brushwood." Their autonym was Quasmigdo.

Biloxi

The Biloxi Tribe are Native Americans of the Siouan language family. They call them-selves by the autonym Tanêks(a) in Siouan Biloxi language. When first encountered by Europeans in 1699, the Biloxi inhabited an area near the coast of the Gulf of Mexico near what is now the city of Biloxi, Mississippi. They were eventually forced west into Louisiana and eastern Texas. The Biloxi language-Tanêksąyaa ade--has been extinct since the 1930s, when the last known native semi-speaker, Emma Jackson, died. Today, remaining Biloxi descendants have merged with the Tunica and other remnant peoples. They were federally recognized in 1981 as the Tunica-Biloxi Tribe of Louisiana and share a small reservation. The two main Tribes were from different language groups. Today the Tribe members speak English or French.

Bisaya

The Bisaya are an indigenous people of the north-west and the coast line of Borneo, Malaysia. They mostly live near the Beaufort district, the river Padas in the Sabah region and along the river Limbang in the northern state Sarawak.

Black Carib (See Garifuna)

Blackfoot and Blackfeet (Also see Niitsítapi)

The Blackfoot Confederacy is the name given to four Native American Tribes in the Northwestern Plains, which include the North Peigan, the South Peigan, the Blood and the Siksika Tribes. In the beginning they occupied a large territory stretching from the North Saskatchewan River in Canada to the Missouri River in Montana. The Piegan Blackfeet are located on the Blackfeet Nation in northwestern Montana near Browning. The other three Tribes are primarily located in Alberta, Canada.

Blood Tribe or Bloods (See Kainai)

Blueberry River First Nation

Blueberry River First Nations was given this name because of the abundant supply of blueberries found in the valley by the river. Blueberry River First Nations is covered under Treaty 8. This community was recognized as the St. John Beaver Band in 1950. The following are the other signatories of Treaty 8: Doig River First Nation, Halfway River First Nation, Prophet River First Nation, West Moberly First Nation, Fort Nel-son First Nation, and McLeod Lake First Nation.

BOḰEĆEN (See Pauquachin)

Bora

The Bora are an indigenous Tribe of the Peruvian, Colombian and Brazilian Amazon, located between the Putumayo and Napo rivers. The Bora speak a Witotan language and comprise approximately 2,000 people. In the last forty years, they have become a largely settled people living mostly in permanent forest settlements. In the animist Bora worldview, there is no distinction between the physical and spiritual worlds and spirits are present throughout the world.

Bribri

The Bribri are an indigenous people of Costa Rica. They live in the Talamanca (can-ton) in Limón Province of Costa Rica. They speak the Bribri language and Spanish.

Brulé

The Brulé are one of the seven branches or bands (sometimes called "sub-tribes") of the Teton (Titonwan) Lakota Sioux American Indian nation. They are known as Sičháŋǧu Oyáte (in Lakota), or "Burnt Thighs Nation," and so, were called Brulé (lit. "burnt") by the French. (The name may have derived from an incident where they

were fleeing through a grass fire on the plains.)

Buryat

The Buryats, numbering approximately 500,000, are the largest indigenous group in Siberia, mainly concentrated in their homeland, the Buryat Republic, a federal subject of Russia. They are the major northern subgroup of the Mongols. Buryats share many customs with other Mongols, including nomadic herding, and erecting gers (yurts) for shelter. Today, the majority of Buryats live in and around Ulan-Ude, the capital of the republic, although many live more traditionally in the countryside. They speak in a dialect of Mongol language called Buryat.

Caddo

The Caddo Nation, originally part of the Hasinai Confederacy, traditionally inhabited much of what is now East Texas, northern Louisiana and portions of southern Arkan-sas and Oklahoma. The state of Texas takes its name from the Spanish spelling of the Caddo word for the confederacy – Tejas – meaning 'those who are friends.'

Cahita

Cáhita is a group of indigenous peoples of Mexico, which includes the Yaqui and Mayo people. Numbering approximately 40,000, they live in west coast of the states of Sonora and Sinaloa. Their language belongs to the Taracahitic family. Cáhita is an agglutinative language, where words use suffix complexes for a variety of purposes with several morphemes strung together.

Cahto

The Cahto (also spelled Kato) are an indigenous Californian group of Native Ameri-cans. Today they are enrolled as the federally recognized Tribe, the Cahto Indian Tribe of the Laytonville Rancheria. A small group of Cahto are enrolled in the Round Valley Indian Tribes of the Round Valley Reservation. Cahto is a Northern Pomo word, meaning "lake", which referred to an important Cahto village site, called Djilbi. The Kato are sometimes referred to as the Kaipomo or Kato people.

Cahuilla

The Cahuilla, Iviatim in their own language, are Native Americans of the inland areas of southern California. Their original territory included an area of about 2,400 square miles (6,200 square km). The traditional Cahuilla territory was near the geographic center of Southern California

Calapooya (See Kalapuya)

Calusa (Caloosa)

The Calusa were a Native American people who lived on the coast and along the inner waterways of Florida's southwest coast. Calusa society developed from that of archaic peoples of the Everglades region; at the time of European contact, the Calusa were the people of the Caloosahatchee culture. They were notable for having devel-oped a complex culture based on estuarine fisheries rather than agriculture.

Carcross/Tagish

For thousands of years the Carcross/Tagish First Nation people have lived off the land and used it's resources to sustain their lives. In order to survive everyone had to work hard. Hunting, fishing, trapping, gathering traditional medicines and berries are still important and part of the First Nation's lifestyle today. It is important to note that the Carcross/Tagish First Nation uses and still maintains many trails within Southern Yukon, Alaska and Northern British Columbia, which includes the famous Chilkoot Trail. The Chilkoot Trail was a trading route long before the arrival of European peo-ples that is part of Carcross/Tagish First Nation Traditional Territory. (Source: http://ctfn.ca/our-people/23-people-culture-history/88-culture-heritage-p6)

Carib

Carib, Island Carib, or Kalinago people, after whom the Caribbean was named, are a group of people who live in the Lesser Antilles islands. They are an Amerindian people whose origins lie in the southern West Indies and the northern coast of South America.

Carquin (also Karkin) (See Ohlone)

Carrier (See Dakelh)

Catawba

The Catawba — also known as Issa or Esaw, but most commonly Iswa, live in the Southeast United States, along the border between North and South Carolina near the city of Rock Hill. The Catawba were once considered one of the most powerful Southeastern Siouan-speaking Tribes.

Cayuga

The Cayuga, "People of the Great Swamp", were one of the five original Nations of the Haudenosaunee (Iroquois) Confederacy – This confederacy was credited by Ben Franklin and Thomas Jefferson as the inspiration for the American Constitution. The Cayuga homeland lays in the Finger Lakes region along Cayuga Lake, between their league neighbours, the Onondaga to the east and the Seneca to the west. Today Cayuga people belong to the Six Nations of the Grand River First Nation in Ontario, the Cayuga Nation of New York and the Seneca-Cayuga Tribe of Oklahoma.

Cayuse

The Cayuse are a Native American Tribe in the state of Oregon. The Cayuse share a reservation in northeastern Oregon with the Umatilla and the Walla Walla Tribes as part of the Confederated Tribes of the Umatilla Indian Reservation. The Cayuse call themselves the Tetawken, which means "we, the people"

Chahta (See Choctaw)

Chappaquiddick

Chappaquiddick, "separated island", the island was once mainly the home territory of the Chappaquiddick band of Wampanoag Indians, remaining exclusively theirs well into the nineteenth century. They still have a reservation of about 100 acres (40 hectares) of brush land in the interior.

Chawathil First Nation

The Chawathil First Nation or Chawathil Indian Band is a band government of the Sto:lo people located in the Upper Fraser Valley region near Hope, British Columbia, Canada. They are a member government of the Stó:lō Tribal Council.

Chawchila (See Chowchila)

Cheam

The Cheam Indian Band is a band government of the Sto:lo people located in the Upper Fraser Valley region of British Columbia, Canada, located near the community of Rosedale. They traditionally speak the Upriver dialect of Halkomelem, one of the Salishan family of languages. The name Cheam means "wild strawberry place" and is the namesake of Mount Cheam, which overlooks the community and most of the Upper Fraser Valley. They are a member government of the Sto:lo Tribal Council, one of two Sto:lo tribal councils. The band services two reserves on the north shore of Cheam Lake, home to 154 people with another 141 living off the reserve.

Chehalis (In Canada See Sts'ailes – in US see Chehlais Tribe below)

Chehalis Tribe (United States)

For many centuries, two large groups of Salish-speaking people lived along the Chehalis River. They lived in cedar longhouses with one end open to the water from which they received a bounty of salmon and other river-based sustenance.
These two groups were the Upper and Lower Chehalis, and they thrived for a long time, until the encroachment of white settlers forced them to give up their ancestral lands. Rejecting the unacceptable terms of the treaties offered by the US Government, the Chehalis were regarded as a "non-treaty" tribe. This meant financial aid from the government would be limited and unpredictable. Despite these challenges, the Chehalis people have endured through self-reliance and determination. Today, the Tribe operates thriving enterprises such as the Lucky Eagle Casino and Eagles Landing Hotel, and has recently built new community and wellness centers that have dramatically enhanced the quality of life for our people. (Source: http://chehalistribe.org/)

Chelan

The Chelan Tribe (pronounced sha-lan), meaning "Deep Water" are an Interior Salish people speaking the Wenatchi dialect, though separate from that Tribe. The Chelan were historically located at the outlet of Lake Chelan in Washington, where they spent the winter months. The Chelan are thought to have splintered off from the Wenatchi Tribe.

Chemainus (See Stz'uminus)

Chemehuevi

As part of the Great Basin Culture Area, the Chemehuevi (a Mojave term meaning "those that play with fish"), a branch of the Southern Paiute, have been persistent occupants of the Mojave Desert. Known to themselves as Nuwu, (The People) they have been nomadic residents of the Mojave Desert's mountains and canyons and the Colorado River shoreline for thousands of years. (Source: chemehuevi.net/)

Cheraw

Believed to be extinct - In 1738, a smallpox epidemic decimated both the Cheraw and the Catawba. The remnants of the two Tribes combined. At some point, some of the Tribe may have moved north and founded the "Charraw Settlement" along Drowning Creek, (present-day Robeson County) North Carolina. The Tribe was mostly destroyed before the middle of the 18th century.

Cheroenhaka

The Cheroenhaka (Nottoway) Indian Tribe, made first ethno-historic contact with the English in 1607/1608 in what is now Nottoway County. We were referred to as Mangoak, or Mengwe, by the Algonquian Tribes and later in 1650, per the diary entries of Edward Bland, referred to again by the Algonquian Tribes as "Nadawa," which soon reverted to Nottoway. In our native Iroquoian Tongue (Dar-sun-ke) we call ourselves CHE-RO-EN-HA-KA – People at the Fork of the Stream. (Source: cheroenhaka-nottoway.org/)

Cherokee (Also see Aniyunwiya)

Since the earliest contact with European explorers in the 16th century, the Cherokee people have been consistently identified as one of the most socially and culturally advanced of the Native American Tribes. Cherokee culture thrived many hundreds of years before initial European contact in the southeastern area of what is now the United States. Cherokee society and culture continued to develop, progressing and embracing cultural elements from European settlers. The Cherokee shaped a government and a society matching the most civilized cultures of the day.

'Trail of Tears' - The Cherokee were herded at bayonet point in a forced march of 1,000 miles ending with our arrival in "Indian Territory", which is today part of the state of Oklahoma. Thousands died in the internment camps, along the trail itself and even after their arrival due to the effects of the journey. (Source: cherokee.org)

Cheslatta Carrier Nation

The Cheslatta Carrier Nation is a First Nation located in the Interior of British Columbia. The traditional territory is centered on Cheslatta Lake. However, much of their territory, including Cheslatta Village, was flooded due to the construction of the Kenney Dam in 1952.

Chetco

The Chetco are a Tribe of Native Americans who originally lived along the lower Chetco River in Curry County in the U.S. state of Oregon. The name Chetco comes from the word meaning "close to the mouth of the stream" in their own language, which is part of the Athapascan languages.

Cheyenne

Cheyenne are an indigenous people of the Great Plains, who are of the Algonquian language family. The Cheyenne Nation is composed of two Tribes, the Só'taeo'o (more commonly spelled as Suhtai or Sutaio) and the Tsétsêhéstâhese (more commonly spelled as Tsitsistas). These merged to form a unified Nation in the early 19th century. Today Cheyenne people are split geographically with the Southern Cheyenne in Oklahoma and the Northern Cheyenne in Montana.

Chickamauga

The Chickamauga Cherokee, also known as the Lower Cherokee, were a band of Cherokee who supported Great Britain at the outbreak of the American Revolutionary War. In 1776/1777, followers of the Cherokee Chief Dragging Canoe, moved with him down the Tennessee River away from the historic Overhill Cherokee towns. In this more isolated area, they established almost a dozen new towns to gain distance from colonists' encroachment. The frontier people often referred to the people as "Chickamaugas," after the name of the new town on the Chickamauga River where Dragging Canoe resided.

After the Cherokee moved further west and southwest five years later, they were more commonly known as the "Lower Cherokee," after the "Five Lower Towns," whose people originally formed the new settlement. Neither they nor other Cherokee considered them separate from the 19th-century Cherokee people.

Chickasaw

From our migration to what is now Mississippi, Kentucky, Alabama and Tennessee in prehistoric times to the purchase of our new homeland in south-central Oklahoma in the mid 1800's, the Chickasaw culture and heritage have always had roots in nature and the elements. With the spirits of our forefathers, we possess a proud history as fierce warriors, known as the "Unconquered and Unconquerable" Chickasaw Nation. (Source: The Official Site of the Chickasaw Nation - chickasaw.net/)

Chicora

The Chicora Tribe was a small Native American Tribe of the Pee Dee area in north-eastern South Carolina, ranging to the Cape Fear River in North Carolina. Scholars consider them a Catawban group, likely to have spoken a Siouan language. Remnants of the Tribe are centered in Conway, South Carolina and are seeking official recognition by the state.

Chilcotin (See Tsilhqot'in)

Chilula

The Chilula were an Athapaskan Tribe who inhabited the area on or near lower Redwood Creek, in Northern California, some 500 to 600 years before contact with Europeans. The Chilula have since been incorporated into the Hoopa Tribe and live mainly on the Hoopa Reservation. The Tribes originally had 18 villages: Howunakut, Noleding, Tlochime, Kingkyolai, Kingyukyomunga, Yisining'aikut, Tsinsilading, Tondinunding, Yinukanomitseding, Hontetlme, Tlocheke, Hlichuhwinauhwding, Kailuhwtahding, Kailuhwchengetlding, Sikingchwungmitahding, Kinahontahding, Misme, and Kahustahding.

Chimariko

The Chimariko were an indigenous people of California, who primarily lived in a narrow, 20-mile section of canyon on the Trinity River in Trinity County in northwestern California. Originally hunter-gatherers, the Chimariko are possibly the earliest residents of their region. They had good relations with Wintu people and were enemies of the Hupa, a Southern Athabaskan people.

Chinook

Chinook refers to several groups of First Nations and Native Americans in the Pacific Northwest region of Canada and the United States, speaking the Chinookan languages. In the early 19th century, the Chinookan-speaking peoples lived along the lower and middle Columbia River in present-day Oregon and Washington. Chinook is also the name of the trade language that was common in the 19th Century.

Chipewyan

The Chipewyan (Denésoliné or Dënesųłiné – "People of the barrens") are a Dene Aboriginal people in Canada, whose ancestors were the Taltheilei. They are part of the Na-dene Athabascan group of people.

Chippewa (See Ojibwe)

Chiricahua Apache

The Chiricahua Nation are a self-sufficient and free people. All the Nation's assets remain traditionally based with a growing international membership and circle of friends. The Ndeh Nation seeks the support and prayers of Earth citizens in the reestablishment of our international status as a Nation in global communities. May our paths be clear and strong. Our culture is our identity, practicing the culture and, teaching the traditions, giving back to humankind we are the Nation. We hold no racial decree nor create dividing lines. The Way of life returns. (Source: http://chiricahuaapache.org/)

Chitimacha

The Chitimacha (also known as "Chetimachan") are a Native American federally recognized Tribe that lives in the U.S. state of Louisiana, mainly in St. Mary Parish. They currently number about 720 people. The Chitimacha language is a language isolate. Chitimacha means warrior. The Chitimacha's historic home was the southern Louisiana coast. They and their ancestors lived there for about 2,500 years and perhaps as long as 6,000. They had migrated from the area surrounding modern Natchez, Mississippi and before that from eastern Texas.

Choctaw

The Choctaw are native to the Southeastern United States and members of the Muskogean linguistic family, which traces its roots to a mound-building, maize-based society that flourished in the Mississippi River Valley for more than a thousand years before European contact. (Source: choctawnation.com/)

Choinumni

Choinumni are one of the many tribes of Yokuts Indians that lived in the San Joaquin Valley of California. The Choinumni lived on the Kings River.

Chontal

The Chontal Maya are an indigenous people of the Mexican state of Tabasco. "Chontal", from the Nahuatl word for chontalli, which means "foreigner", has been applied to various ethnic groups in Mexico. The Chontal refer to themselves as the Yokot'anob or the Yokot'an, meaning "the speakers of Yoko ochoco", but writers about them refer to them as the Chontal of Centla, the Tabasco Chontal, or in Spanish, Chontales. They consider themselves the descendants of the Olmecs, and are not related to the Oaxacan Chontal.

Chowchilla

The Chowchilla lived along the several channels of the Chowchilla River in the plains region of Central California. According to one authority, the Chowchilla Tribe may well have been a very populous Tribe. At least we know they were a warlike one and the name Chowchilla was a byword for bravery to the southernmost end of Yokuts territory in the southern end of the San Joaquin Valley. (Source: http://ci.chowchilla.ca.us/city%20facts/history.htm)

Chukchansi

The Chukchansi people are one of the original inhabitants of what now is called California. The Chukchansi have inhabited the fringes of the San Joaquin Valley and the foothills of the Sierra Nevada for more than 12,000 years. During the years after the Gold Rush (1849), anthropologists visited the land of the Chukchansi. They grouped California Tribes together by their languages; hence, the Chukchansi are grouped with approximately 60 other Tribes in the greater Central Valley. These groups had (and still have) similar cultures, and speak the same language, but had different dialects. (Source: chukchansi.net/history.html)

Chumash

The Chumash are a Native American people who historically inhabited the central and southern coastal regions of California extending from Morro Bay in the north to Malibu in the south. They also occupied three of the Channel Islands.

Clackamas

The Clackamas Indians are a Tribe of Native Americans of the U.S. state of Oregon who traditionally lived along the Clackamas River in the Willamette Valley. Lewis and Clark estimated their population at 1800 in 1806. By 1855, the 88 surviving members of the Tribe were relocated to Grand Ronde, Oregon, first to the Grand Ronde Indian Reservation; later they blended into the general population. Descendants of the Clackamas belong to the Confederated Tribes of the Grand Ronde Community of Oregon.

Clatskanie

Clatskanie (Kwalhioqua, Tlatskanie, Klaatshan). Kwalhioqua-Clatskanie was an Athabascan language once spoken by the Willapa, Suwal, and Clatskanie Tribes of Oregon and Washington state. These Tribes were decimated by smallpox in the early 1800's, and the survivors merged into neighbouring Tribes. Though there are still Clatskanie and Kwahlioqua descendents among other Tribes of northwest Oregon, they have not survived as distinct Nations, and the language has not been spoken since the 1930's. (Source: native-languages.org/clatskanie.htm)

Clatsop-Nehalem

From the very earliest written record of the Clatsop and Nehalem people, they are described as being culturally, economically, and socially integrated with one another. Most Clatsops dwelled along the northern Oregon coast from the Columbia River to Tillamook Head near Seaside, while most Nehalem-Tillamook dwelled in villages from there to well south of Tillamook Bay. Though their languages were different, Clatsops and Nehalems were bilingual. (Source: The Official Site of the Clatsop-Nehalem Confederated Tribes - clatsop-nehalem.com/history.html)

Cochimí

The Cochimí are the Aboriginal inhabitants of the central part of the Baja California peninsula, from El Rosario in the north to San Javier in the south.

Cochiti

The Pueblo de Cochiti, (Cochiti), is located 55 miles north of Albuquerque, New Mexico. The people of Cochiti continue to retain their native language of Keres. They are well known for their craftsmanship in storytelling and making jewelry, pottery, and drums. (Source: The Official Website of the Cochiti Pueblo - pueblodecochiti.org/)

Cocopah

The Cocopah Tribe is one of seven descendant Tribes from the greater Yuman language-speaking people who occupied lands along the Colorado River. Cocopah Tribal ancestors also lived along the Lower Colorado River region near the river delta and the Gulf of California. The Cocopah people had no written language, however, historical records were passed on orally or interpreted in documents written by outside visitors. (Source: cocopah.com/about-us.html)

Coeur d'Alene

The Coeur d'Alene are a Native American people who lived in what is now northern Idaho, eastern Washington and western Montana. In their language, members call themselves Schitsu'umsh (or Skitswish), meaning The Discovered People or Those Who Are Found Here. French Canadian fur traders in the late 18th or early 19th century gave them their non-native name.

Cofan

The Cofan people are an indigenous people native to northeast Ecuador and southern Colombia. They speak the Cofán language or A'ingae, a language of the Chibchan family. The ancestral land, community health and social cohesion of Cofan communities in Ecuador has been severely damaged by several decades of oil drilling.

Coharie

The Coharie Tribe is located in the State of North Carolina in the counties of Harnett and Sampson. They descend from the Aboriginal Tribe of the Neusiok Indians. Historical movements, initiated by Inter-Tribal conflicts as well as White/Native colonial hostilities, caused the Coharies to move to their present location between 1729 and 1746. (Source: coharieTribe.org/)

Coldwater First Nation

Coldwater First Nation is a Nlaka'pamux First Nations government located in the Central Interior region of the Canadian province of British Columbia. It is a member of the Nicola Tribal Association, which are two of three tribal councils of the Nlaka'pamux people. Other Nlaka'pamux governments belong either to the Fraser Canyon Indian Administration or the Nlaka'pamux Nation Tribal Council.

Columbia (See Sinkiuse-Columbia)

Colville

The Colville is a Native American Tribe of the Pacific Northwest. The name Colville comes from association with Fort Colville. Earlier, outsiders often named the Colville Scheulpi or Chualpay; the French traders called them Les Chaudières ("the kettles") in reference to Kettle Falls. The Tribe's history is tied with Kettle Falls, an important salmon fishing resource.

Comanche

The Comanche are a Plains Indian tribe whose historic territory, known as Comancheria, consisted of present day eastern New Mexico, southern Colorado, northeastern Arizona, southern Kansas, all of Oklahoma, and most of northwest Texas. The Comanche people are federally recognized as the Comanche Nation, with a reservation and headquarters in Lawton, Oklahoma. The Comanche spoke the Comanche language, a Numic language of the Uto-Aztecan family, sometimes classified as a Shoshone dialect. Historically, the Comanches were hunter-gatherers with a horse culture. There may have been as many as 45,000 Comanches in the late 18th century. Today, the Comanche Nation has 15,191 members, with approximately 7,763 members residing in the Lawton – Fort Sill and surrounding areas of Southwest Oklahoma.

Comcaac (See Seri)

Comox (See K'ómoks)

Conestoga (See Susquehannock)

Confederated Tribes of Coos, Siuslaw and Lower Umpqua

The Confederated Tribes of Coos, Lower Umpqua, and Siuslaw Indians trace their ancestry back to the Aboriginal inhabitants of the South-Central coast of Oregon. Their historic homelands extended from the Coastal Range in the East to the Pacific Ocean in the West, a region of some 1.6 million acres. They lived peacefully in an area characterized by moderate temperatures and abundant natural resources, including fish, shellfish, wildlife, and a rich variety of edible plants. (Source: http://ctclusi.org/

Conoy (See Piscataway)

Constance Lake First Nation

Constance Lake First Nation is an Oji-Cree First Nation in Cochrane District in northeastern Ontario, directly north of the community of Calstock. As a signatory to Treaty 9, the First Nation is a member of Matawa First Nations, a Regional Chiefs' Council; the Regional Chiefs' Council, in turn, is a member of the Nishnawbe Aski Nation, a Tribal Political Organization representing many of the First Nations in Northern and Northwestern Ontario.

Coos (Coosan) (See Confederated Tribes of Coos)

Copper River Athabascan (See Ahtna)

Coquille

The Coquille (or Ko-Kwell) are a Native American Tribe centered in southwest Oregon, where the Coos River flows into Coos Bay. The name of the Coquille is derived from the French, literally translated as "shell." The name was given by French Canadian voyageur trappers working for the North West Company, because of their diet of shellfish and use of shells as personal ornament.

Cora

The Cora (or Chora) are an indigenous ethnic group of Western Central Mexico that live in the Sierra de Nayarit and in La Mesa de Nayar in the Mexican states of Jalisco and Nayarit. They call themselves náayarite, which is where the name of the state is derived from. The Cora cultivate maize, beans, and amaranth and they raise some cattle.

Coso

The Coso are a Native American Tribe associated with the Coso Range in the Mojave Desert of California in the southwestern U.S. They are of the Uto-Aztecan language and spoke one of several Numic languages, related to that of the Northern Paiute. They are especially known for their ancient petroglyphs, or rock art drawings.

Costanoan (See Ohlone)

Coushatta

The Coushatta (Koasati in their own language) are a Muskogean-speaking people living primarily in the U.S. state of Louisiana. When first encountered by Europeans, they lived in Georgia and Alabama. After 1763, they began to move west into Mississippi, Louisiana and Texas. Some of the Coushatta were removed west to Oklahoma in the 1830s together with other Muscogee peoples.

Cowichan

We have owned and occupied our territory for thousands of years. Archaeological evidence dates our existence as long ago as 4,500 years, but our historical memory says that we have been here since time immemorial. While we have evolved into a modern society, many of our cultural practices and traditions have been carried on for generations, and are still woven into our culture today.

The Cowichan Tribes are the single largest First Nations in British Columbia with Over 4500 registered members; about half currently live on the reserve. Located in the Cowichan Valley, in mid-Vancouver Island, British Columbia. Comprised of seven traditional villages: Kw'amutsun, Qwum'yiqun', Hwulqwselu, S'amuna', L'uml'umuluts, Hinupsum, Tl'ulpalus. (Source: http://cowichantribes.com)

Cowlitz

Cowlitz people are an indigenous people of the Northwestern Plateau. Their traditional homelands are in western Washington in the United States. They consist of two distinct groups: the Upper Cowlitz, or Taidnapam, and the Lower Cowlitz, or Kawlic. The original language of Cowlitz Tribes belonged to the Salishan family of languages among Northwest Coast indigenous peoples. Later, the Upper Cowlitz adopted the Sahaptin language from east of the Cascade Mountains.

Cree

The Cree are one of the largest groups of First Nations/Native Americans in North America, with 200,000 members living in Canada. Most live north and west of Lake Superior, in Ontario, Manitoba, Saskatchewan, Alberta and the Northwest Territories though some live in eastern Quebec. In the United States, this Algonquian-speaking people historically lived from Lake Superior westward. Today, they live mostly in Montana, where they share a reservation with the Ojibwe (Chippewa). The documented westward migration over time has been strongly associated with their roles as traders and hunters in the North American Fur Trade.

Creek (See Muscogee)

Croatan

The Croatan were a small Native American group living in the coastal areas of what is now North Carolina. They may have been a branch of the larger Roanoke people or allied with them. The Croatan Indians [Roanoke colony] were a peaceful Tribe that spoke English fluently and practiced Christianity.

Crow (See Apsáalooke)

Cucupa

The Cucupa are an indigenous people from northern Mexico and southern California near the Columbia River. The small tribe is situated 60 miles south of Mexicali along the Rio Hardy, where the tribe's existence is threatened, not only by the loss of traditions and language but also by a lack of viable income.

Cuna (See Kuna)

Cuncos

The Cuncos are a native Chilean people, belonging to the southern group of Mapuche peoples. They spoke the Mapudungun language, common to all the Mapuche peoples.

Cupeño (Cupa)

The Cupeño are a Native American Tribe from Southern California. Their name in their own language is Kuupangaxwichem. They traditionally lived near the modern day U.S.-Mexico border in the Peninsular Range of Southern California. Today they are part of the Pala Band of Luiseno Mission Indians, Morongo Band of Cahuilla Mission Indians, and Los Coyotes Band of Cahuilla and Cupeno Indians.

Cup`ik (See Yup`ik)

Dakelh

The Dakelh or Carrier are the indigenous people of a large portion of the Central Interior of British Columbia, Canada. Most call themselves Dakelh, meaning "people who go around by boat." The term Carrier is a translation of the name for them used by the neighbouring Sekani First Nations people which Europeans learned first because they crossed Sekani territory before entering Carrier territory. The Dakelh are linguistically Athabaskan.

Dakota (See Sioux)

Dakubetede (Applegate, Applegate River Indians)

A small Tribe from the group Athapaska (narrower group Coquille) that settled along the Applegate Creek, in southwest Oregon in the 19th century.

Da'naxda'xw / Awaetlala

The Da'naxda'xw First Nation is an amalgamation of the Da'naxda'xw and Awaetlala tribes of Knight Inlet. The main village of the Da'naxda'xw, Tsatsisnukwomi, is situated at Dead Point on Harbledown Island. This village is in Indian Channel and approximately 25 kilometers east of Alert Bay on the west coast of British Columbia, Canada.

Danezaa (Dunne-za Dane-zaa, Dunneza)

The Danezaa (also spelled Dunneza or Tsattine) are a First Nation of the large Athapaskan language group; their traditional territory is around the Peace River of Alberta and British Columbia. About 1,000 Dane-zaa are living today in British Columbia and perhaps half speak the Danezaa language, and around 2,000 live in Alberta.

Deg Xinag (Deg Hit'an)

Deg Hit'an (also Deg Xit'an, Deg Hitan, Degexit'an, Kaiyuhkhotana) are a group of Northern Athabascan peoples in Alaska. Their native language is called Deg Xinag. They reside along the Anvik River in Anvik, along the Innoko River in Shageluk, and at Holy Cross along the lower Yukon River.

Delaware

This name was given to the people who lived along the Delaware River. It later came to be applied to almost all Lenape people. In their language, which belongs to the Algonquian language family, they are LENAPE (len-NAH-pay) which means something like "The People." They were among the first Native Americans to come in contact with the Europeans and were respected by other Tribes as peacemakers. (Source: http://culture.delawareTribe.org/home.htm)

Dena'ina (Denaina)

The Dena'ina (also Tanaina) are an Alaska Native people and Athabaskan Native Americans in the United States. They are the original inhabitants of the southcentral Alaska region. The name means "the people," and is related to the preferred name for the Navajo people "Dene." The Dena'ina are the only Northern Athabascan group to live on saltwater and this allowed them to have the most sedentary lifestyle of all Northern Athabascans.

Dene (Denesuline)

Dene is the common Athabaskan word for "people" and has two usages. More commonly, it is used narrowly to refer to the Athabaskan speakers of the Northwest Territories and Nunavut in Canada, but it is sometimes also used to refer to all Northern Athabaskan speakers, who are spread in a wide range all across Alaska and northern Canada. Note that Dene never includes the Pacific Coast Athabaskan or Southern Athabaskan speakers in the continental U.S., despite the fact that the term is used to denote the Athabaskan languages as a whole (the Na-Dene language family).

Dene Tha'

The Dene Tha' First Nation is a First Nations government of the South Slavey in Northern Alberta. Its population is centred in three communities: Bushe River, Meander River and Chateh. Dene Tha' is a member of the North Peace Tribal Council

Diegueño (See Kumeyaay)

Dine (Dineh) (Also see Navajo)

The Dine (Dineh) is Na-Dene word that the Navajo call themselves and is the largest North American Tribe. Before moving south (approx. 1000 AD) the Dine lived in Northwestern Canada and Alaska. The Naabeehó Diné'é (Navajo Nation) is the name of a sovereign Native American Nation established by the Diné. The Navajo Nation covers about 27,000 square miles (70,000 square Kilometers) of land, occupying all of northeastern Arizona, and extending into Utah and New Mexico, and is the largest land area assigned primarily to a Native American jurisdiction within the United States.

Ditidaht First Nation

Our Ditidaht territory is large. It stretches inland to include Cowichan Lake. It reaches down Nitinat Lake and deep into the forests. It extends along the coast between Bonilla Point and Pachena Point and encompasses a considerable distance offshore. On the other side of Bonilla Point live our close relatives, the Pacheenaht, and to the northwest of Pachena Point is the country of our neighbours, the Ohiaht who speak a different language.

More generally, Ditidaht territory on land extends to the headwaters of the streams and rivers which drain down to the coastline. Ditidaht territory extends out to sea and includes the rich salmon, halibut and cod banks that feed our people. Ours is a big country that is rich in the foods we like to eat. Every year the salmon come back to rivers like the Cheewhat, Hobarton and Nitinat. We can always get mussels from the rocky coastline and sea urchins in the shallow waters. And there are thousands of crabs scurrying around the lower end of Nitinat Lake, just waiting to be trapped. Deer and elk are in the forests and berries of all types are growing on the hillsides. Ducks are everywhere. People never go hungry in Ditidaht country! (Source: ditidaht.ca/history.htm)

Dogon

The Dogon are an ethnic group living in the central plateau region of the country of Mali, in the West of the Continent of Africa, in the Mopti region. The Dogon are best known for their religious traditions, their mask dances, wooden sculpture and their architecture. An interesting cultural tradition is that the Dogon represented the brightest star in the heavens, Sirius, as twins – modern science only discovered that it was a twin star in the 20th Century. Some use this curious fact as proof that the ancients had a deeper cosmological understanding of the universe than is normally credited.

Dogrib (See Tłı̨chǫ)

Dumna

The Dumna people, who originally lived in the area that is now Fresno and Madera counties, are related to the surrounding Monache tribes. Funds supported costs associated with planning and implementing of a "Dumna Tribal Coming Out Ceremony," which was the first public ceremony to be practiced by the Dumna for over five decades. The gathering provided an opportunity to teach Dumna descendents the history, ceremonies and dances of their people. (Source: dumnaindians.org)

Duwamish (Dkhw'Duw'Absh)

The Duwamish (sometimes referred to as the Suquamish) are a Lushootseed-speaking Native American Tribe, located in present-day Washington in the United States. The Duwamish are a southern Coast Salish people. Like many Northwest Coast natives, the Duwamish relied on fishing from local rivers and Puget Sound for food. They built plank longhouses to protect themselves from the wet winters west of the Cascade Mountains. The people known today as the Duwamish Tribe are the Dkhw'Duw'Absh, "The People of the Inside". We are the people of Chief Seattle. We are the First People of the City of Seattle, Mercer Island, Renton, Bellevue, Tukwila and much of King County, Washington. We have never left our ancestral homeland. We are bringing the strengths of our Native Nation, our culture, our teachings, and our Native values with us into the 21st Century. (Source: http://duwamishtribe.org/culture.html)

Dzawadạ̱'enux̱w

The Dzawadạ̱'enux̱w (Tsawataineuk is the anglicized version) First Nation is a First Nations band government in the Queen Charlotte Strait region north of northern Vancouver Island in the Canadian province of British Columbia. It is a member of the Musgamagw Tsawataineuk Tribal Council, along with the 'Namgis First Nation and the Kwicksutaineuk-ah-kwa-mish First Nation. The territory of the Dzawadạ̱'enux̱w First Nation spans the whole of Broughton Archipelago on the northern side of Queen Charlotte Strait and adjoining areas of the BC mainland. The main village of the Tsawataineuk people is Gwa'Yi, at the mouth of the Kingcome River.

Eansketambawg

The Quinnipiac is the English name for the Eansketambawg (meaning " we, the original, surface-dwelling people") are Native American Nation of the Algonquian family who inhabited the Wampanoki ("Dawnland") region, including present-day Connecticut. In 2000, they published their revised Ancient Laws and Traditions:

"WE, the Indigenous Algonquian People of South western Connecticut known to outsiders as the "Quinnipiac Indians" and/or the "New Haven Tribe of Indians", for ourselves, our descendants, our allies, and in order to inform the general public, as well as all local, state and federal governmental agencies etc. about ourselves… do hereby publish and make available as a matter of public record the millennium (Y2K) revised edition of our Ancient Laws and Covenant Traditions which has served us and our ancestors as guidelines for Self-Government since time immemorial." (Source: http://acqtc.org/Organization/Constitution)

Echota

Members of the Echota Cherokee Tribe of Alabama are the descendants of Cherokees who escaped the Trail of Tears by hiding in the mountains, were able to escape during the march, or returned after being brought to Indian Territory. The language and culture were kept hidden and secret, for fear that if someone found out, they would be taken to Indian Territory and everything they had would be taken by the state. (Source: echotadeerclanwest.com/pages/DCW%20official%20business/History/ECToA%20history.htm)

Edisto (See Natchez)

Eel River

The Eel River are a Native American Tribe who lived in what is today Indiana at the time of European settlement. They are sometimes classified as part of the Miami Indians and are often confused with the Wea Indians and the Pankishaw and Pokias.

Eenou (Eeyou) (See Cree)

Embera-Wounaan

The Embera–Wounaan is a semi-nomadic indigenous people in Panama, living in the province of Darien. The Embera-Wounaan were formerly and widely known by the name Chocó, and they speak the Embera and Wounaan languages, part of the Chocoan language family. The name "Embera" means "people." Collectively they are known as the Chocó and belong to two major groups: the Embirá, of upper Atrato and San Juan Rivers, and the Wuanana of the lower San Juan River. A third group of Chocó are called the Catío.

Erie

The Erie (also Erieehronon, Eriechronon, Riquéronon, Erielhonan, Eriez, Nation du Chat) were a Native American people historically living on the south shore of Lake Erie. An Iroquoian group, they lived in what is now western New York, northwestern Pennsylvania, and northern Ohio. They were decimated by warfare with the neighbouring Iroquois in the 17th century for helping the Hurons, an enemy of the Iroquois. The Erie were absorbed by other Iroquoian tribes, particularly the Seneca, and gradually lost their independent identity. The villages were burned as a lesson to those who dare oppose the Iroquois. The names Erie and Eriez are shortened forms of Erielhonan, meaning "long tail." The Erielhonan were also called the "Cat" or the "Raccoon" people. They lived in multi-family long houses in villages enclosed in palisades. They grew the "Three Sisters": varieties of corn, beans, and squash, during the warm season. In winter, tribal members lived off the stored crops and animals taken in hunts.

Esk'etemc

Esk'etemc is a Secwepemctsin speaking group. Esk'etemc has 19 reserves situated on the Fraser River southwest of Williams Lake, with an approximate total area of 3,800 hectares. Esk'etemc's administrative offices and the majority of the population are located on IR #1 (Esk'et) about 50 kilometres from Williams Lake on the east side of the Fraser River at Alkali Lake. (Source: http://esketemc.org/)

Esquimalt (SXIMEȽEȽ) (See W̱SÁNEC̱)

Esselen

The Esselen are a Native American people belonging to a linguistic group in the hypothetical Hokan language family, indigenous to the Central California coast and the coastal mountains, including what is now known as the Big Sur region in Monterey County, California. The members of this Tribe are currently scattered, but many still live in the Monterey Peninsula and nearby regions.

Etchenin (Etchimin)

The French referred to both the Passamaquoddy and their Maliseet kinfolk by the same name, "Etchimins." They were closely related peoples who shared a common language, but the two Tribes have always considered themselves politically independent. Smallpox and other European diseases took a heavy toll on the Passamaquoddy tribe, which was reduced from at least 20,000 people to no more than 4000. (Source: native-languages.org/passamaquoddy.htm)

Euchee (See Yuchi)

Eudeve (Endeve) (Also see Opata)

At the time of the first contact with the Spanish in the 16th century, there were multiple sub-groups of Opata people. However, by the mid 17th century, the Spanish identified only three Opatan groups. The largest was the Eudeve, (eh-oo-deh-veh), whose ancient villages and current towns encompass the western portions of traditional Opata territory. The Eudeve also referred to themselves for short as "Deve." Both names mean "people."

Evenks

The Evenks are a Tungusic people of Northern Asia. In Russia, the Evenks are recognized as one of the Indigenous peoples of the Russian North, with a population of 35,527 (2002 Census). In China, the Evenki form one of the 56 ethnic groups officially recognized by the People's Republic of China. There are also 535 Mongolized Evenki in Mongolia, referred to as Khamnigan.

Eyak

The Eyak are an indigenous group traditionally located on the Copper River Delta and near the town of Cordova, Alaska.

Fernandeño /Tataviam

The Fernandeño Tataviam's region stretches from the San Fernando Valley and Santa Clarita Valley (California) to the Antelope Valley and can be traced as far back as 450 A.D. At that time the Tataviam people migrated from the north and settled in villages throughout the area. The villages were constructed on the south-facing sides of hills and mountains because they received the most sunlight. The word Tataviam means "people facing the sun" and describes the Tataviam villages. (Source: http://tataviam-nsn.us/)

Flathead Salish

The Confederated Salish and Kootenai Tribes of the Flathead Indian Reservation are the modern representatives of several Salish, Kootenai and Pend O'Reilles bands who lived in western Montana, northern Idaho, and eastern Washington in the early 1800s. Before the arrival of Europeans, the tribal people hunted and gathered plants over an area the size of many eastern states. Twice a year, they made cooperative hunting trips over the Continental Divide to the buffalo herds of the Great Plains. (Source: http://lakecodirect.com/archives/The_Flathead_Nation.html)

Fond du Lac

The Fond du Lac Band of Lake Superior Chippewa Reservation lies in Northeastern Minnesota adjacent to the city of Cloquet, MN, approximately 20 miles west of Duluth, MN. The Fond du Lac Reservation, established by the LaPointe Treaty of 1854, is one of six Reservations inhabited by members of the Minnesota Chippewa Tribe. The Chippewa Nation is the second largest ethnic group of Native Americans in the United States. Archaeologists maintain that ancestors of the present day Chippewa have resided in the Great Lakes area since at least 800 A.D. (Source: http://fdlrez.com/)

Fort Nelson First Nation

The Fort Nelson First Nation (FNFN) reserve is located 7 km's south of the town of Fort Nelson in the northeastern corner of British Columbia; the community is located at Mile 293-295 on the Alaska Highway. The Nation is a Slavey/Cree linguistic group with roughly 638 band members living on and off reserve. The FNFN is one of 6 First Nation's that belong to Treaty 8. (Source: http://fortnelsonfirstnation.org/)

Fox (See Meskwaki)

Gabrielino (Gabrieleno) (See Kizh)

Gaigwu (See Kiowa)

Galibi (See Kali'na)

Garifuna

The Garifuna are descendants of Carib, Arawak and West African people. Today the Garifuna live primarily in Central America, along the Caribbean Coast in Belize, Guatemala, Nicaragua and Honduras including the mainland, and on the island of Roatán. There are also diaspora communities of Garifuna in the United States, particularly in Los Angeles, Miami, New York and other major cities.

Gashowu (See Yokuts)

Gila River (See Pima)

Gitga'at

From the beginning of time, the Gitga'at people have existed in their Territory on what is now British Columbia's northwest coast. The wellbeing of their people is intricately related to the health of their lands, waters, and resources, and the community continues to work to sustain their abundance and richness. Gitga'at culture is strengthening, and traditional practices continue to shape day to day life in the village. (Source: http://gitgaat.net/)

Gitxaala First Nation

The Gitxaala Nation is a First Nations government located at Kitkatla, British Columbia, Canada in the province's North Coast region. It is one of the longest continually inhabited communities in all of "Turtle Island" which is a reference to all of North America. The ancestry of the people living here dates back to 10,000 years! It is a beautiful and peaceful community that values and respects the ideal location and resources on which the people and animals have lived for centuries. (Source: http://gitxaalanation.com/)

Gitxsan (Gitksan)

The Gitxsan pre-contact economy was based on the trading of salmon, other natural resources, and products/goods derived from these resources. Lots of trading occurred along grease trails with neighbouring coastal First Nations for oolichan (candle fish) grease. The Gitxsan had a well-organized society pre-contact with political, social, legal and economic institutions based on the Huwilp (House groups). Gitxsan institutions based on natural law, balanced lifestyle, respect, and obligation to the community, which governed pre-contact Gitxsan society continue to be at work today. Since contact the Gitxsan have always asserted ownership of, jurisdiction over, and the right to self-government on, Gitxsan Territory (Lax Yip). (Source: http://gitxsan.com/about/our-history/pre-contact/)

Goshute

The Goshutes are a band of Western Shoshone Native Americans. There are two federally recognized Goshute tribes today: the Confederated Tribes of the Goshute Reservation and Skull Valley Band of Goshute Indians of Utah of the Skull Valley Indian Reservation. The name Goshute derived either from a leader named Goship or from Gutsipupiutsi, a Shoshone word for Desert People.

Grand Ronde

The Confederated Tribes of the Grand Ronde Community of Oregon consists of twenty-seven Native American tribes with long historical ties to present-day Western Oregon between the western boundary of the Oregon Coast and the eastern boundary of the Cascade Range, and the northern boundary of southwestern Washington, and the southern boundary of Northern California. (Source: grandronde.org)

Gros Ventre

The Gros Ventre people (from French: big belly), also known as the A'ani, A'aninin, Haaninin, and Atsina, are an Algonquian-speaking Native American Tribe located in north central Montana. A'ani, A'aninin, and Haaninin are the Tribe's autonyms. These terms mean "White Clay People" or "Lime People." The French used the term Gros Ventre, which was mistakenly interpreted from their sign language.

Guarani

Guarani are a group of culturally related indigenous peoples of South America. They are distinguished from the related Tupi by their use of the Guarani language. Their traditional range is in Paraguay, Argentina, southern Brazil, and parts of Uruguay and Bolivia. The Guarani language is one of the two official languages in Paraguay, the other one being Spanish.

Guarijio

An indigenous people of Mexico, the Guarijio are divided into two groups, the Sonoran and the Chihuahua. The latter has merged with the Tarahumara and adopted their customs. Despite the common cultural heritage, there are no relations between the two Guarijio groups today, and they have developed dialectal variations; the Guarijio of Sonora can now communicate better in their maternal language with the Mayo than with the Guarijio of Chihuahua. Those of Sonora now call themselves "the real Guarijio". (Source: everyculture.com/Middle-America-Caribbean/Guarij-o-History-and-Cultural-Relations.html

Gwich'in

The Gwich'in (sometimes rendered as Kutchin or Gwitchin), literally "one who dwells" or "resident of [a region]", are a First Nations/Alaska Native people who live in the northwestern part of North America mostly above the Arctic Circle. Gwich'in often self-reference using the term "Dinjii Zhuu" instead of Gwich'in. The Gwich'in are well known for the construction of snowshoes, birchbark canoes, the two-way sled, and intricate and ornate beadwork. Traditional caribou skin clothing and porcupine quill sewing are also held in high regard among Gwich'in.

Hadzabe

The Hadzabe, or Hadza, are an ethnic group in north-central Tanzania, living around Lake Eyasi in the central Rift Valley and in the neighbouring Serengeti Plateau. Some Hadza still live as hunter-gatherers, they are the last full-time hunter-gatherers in Africa. The Hadza are not closely genetically related to any other people. While traditionally classified with the Khoisan languages, primarily because it has clicks, the Hadza language appears to be an isolate, unrelated to any other.

Haida

Haida people have occupied Haida Gwaii since time immemorial. Our traditional territory encompasses parts of southern Alaska, the archipelago of Haida Gwaii and its surrounding waters. Our pre-contact population was in the tens of thousands in several dozen towns dispersed throughout the islands. During the time of contact our population fell to about 600, this was due to introduced disease including measles, typhoid and smallpox.

Today, Haida people make up half of the 5000 people living on the islands. Haida reside throughout the islands but are concentrated in two main centres, Old Massett at the north end of Graham Island and Skidegate at the south end. Besides these two communities there are many 2000 more Haida scattered throughout the world. Vancouver, 770 km south of Haida Gwaii, has a large population as does Prince Rupert which is 100 km east across Hecate Srait. The Haida Nation collectively holds Hereditary and Aboriginal Title and Rights to Haida Territories and the cultural and intellectual property rights of the Haida Nation. (Source: http://haidanation.ca/Pages/history/haidanation.html)

Haisla

In 1918, an influenza pandemic dramatically reduced the Haisla population and wiped out the Wolf and Frog clans. The Haisla community recovered and continues to evolve. Today there are about 1500 Haisla, half of which live in Kitamaat Village. Though clan distinctions and connections remain today, Haisla culture combines traditional heritage with Canadian culture. The Na Na Kila Institute was established in 1998 to help protect and encourage development of Haisla culture, including language. Na Na Kila helped bring about the repatriation of a Haisla totem pole that had been removed in 1929 and was missing for more than 60 years. It was discovered in the Museum of Ethnography in Stockholm in 1991 and, after years of negotiation, it was returned to Kitamaat on July 1, 2006. As part of the agreement the Haisla carved a replica pole for the museum in Stockholm. (Source; http://haisla.ca)

Halfway River First Nation

Halfway River First Nation is a Dunneza First Nations government with a 3988 hectare reserve located 75 km northwest of Fort St. John, British Columbia. It is a Treaty 8 nation. The Halfway River people were at one point part of the "Hudson Hope Indian Band" but in 1971 they split off, and the remaining people formed West Moberly First Nations. As of January 2008, there were 235 registered members, with 132 living on the reserve.

Hän

The Hän (also Hankutchin or Han) are a Northern Athabascan people who speak the Hän language. Only a handful of fluent speakers remain. Their traditional land centered around a heavily forested area around the Yukon River straddling what is now the Alaska-Yukon Territory border. The name Han is a shortening of Hankutchin, which is the Gwich'in word for the Hän, literally meaning "people of the river."

Hanis (See Coos)

Hare (See Sahtu)

Hasinai

The Hasinai Confederacy (Caddo: Hasíinay) was a large confederation of Caddo-speaking Native Americans located between the Sabine and Trinity rivers in eastern Texas. Today they are enrolled in the Caddo Nation of Oklahoma.

Haudenosaunee (Confederacy)

The Haudenosaunee (more commonly known as the Iroquois) or the "People of the Longhouse", are a league of several Nations and Tribes of indigenous people of North America. After the Iroquoian-speaking peoples of present-day central and upstate New York coalesced as distinct Tribes, they came together in an association known today as the Iroquois League, or the "League of Peace and Power." The original Iroquois League was often known as the Five Nations, as it was composed of the Mohawk, Oneida, Onondaga, Cayuga, and Seneca Nations.

August 31, 1142. According to research by Barbara Mann and Jerry Fields of Toledo University, Ohio they state that the Seneca, the last to adopt the 'Great Law of Peace' did so shortly after a solar eclipse. This makes the Haudenosaunee (Iroquois) Confederacy as one of the oldest continuing running democracies in the world. After the Tuscarora Nation joined the League in 1722, the Iroquois became known as the Six Nations.

Havasupai

Havasupai means "people of the blue green water." Havasupais have dwelt in the Grand Canyon and the rest of north-central Arizona for over 1,000 years, practicing summertime irrigated farming in the canyons and wintertime hunting in the plateaus. The Tribe is known for its location, traditional cultural life, and beautiful arts and crafts. (Source: The Official Website of the Havasupai Tribe - http://havasupai-nsn.gov/)

Hawaiian (See Kānaka Maoli)

Heiltsuk

The Heiltsuk or (more commonly - Bella Bella) are an Indigenous First Nations of the Central Coast region of the Canadian province of British Columbia, centered on the island communities of Bella Bella and Klemtu. The government of the Heiltsuk people is the Heiltsuk Nation. Its largest community is Bella Bella.

Heve (See Opata)

Hiaki (See Yaqui)

Hidatsa

The Hidatsa (called Minnetaree by their allies) are a Siouan people, a part of the Three Affiliated Tribes. The Hidatsa's autonym is Hiraacá. According to the Tribal tradition, the word hiraacá derives from the word "willow." The present name Hidatsa was formerly borne by one of the three tribal villages. When the villages consolidated, the name was adopted for the Tribe as a whole. Their language is related to that of the Crow, and they are sometimes considered a parent Tribe to the modern Crow in Montana.

Hitchiti

The Hitchiti were an indigenous tribe formerly residing in western present-day Georgia. They spoke the Hitchiti language, which was part of the Muskogean language family; it is considered a dialect of the Mikasuki language, with which it was mutually intelligible.

Hmong

The Hmong are an Asian ethnic group from the mountainous regions of China, Vietnam, Laos, and Thailand. Hmong are also one of the sub-groups of the Miao ethnicity in southern China. Hmong groups began a gradual southward migration in the 18th century due to political unrest and to find more arable land. Hmong are rich in culture, art and family and are distinguished by costume/dress (fabric patterns represent fruit, vegetables, farming, chickens, eggs, etc.).

Ho-Chunk

The Ho-Chunk, also known as Winnebago, is a Siouan-speaking Tribe of Native Americans, native to the present-day states of Wisconsin, Minnesota, and parts of Iowa and Illinois. Today the two federally recognized Ho-Chunk Tribes, the Ho-Chunk Nation of Wisconsin and Winnebago Tribe of Nebraska, have territory primarily within the states included in their names. The Ho-Chunk was the dominant Tribe

in their territory in the sixteenth century.

Hohe (See Nakoda)

Holikachuk

Holikachuk (also Innoko, Organized Village of Grayling, Innoka-khotana, Tlëgon-khotana) are an Athabaskan people native to western Alaska. The Holikachuk call themselves "Doogh Hit'an". The name Holikachuk is derived from the name (in the Holikachuk language) of a village in native Holikachuk territory.

Homalco

The Homalco First Nation is located in Bute Inlet near the upper Sunshine Coast of British Columbia, Canada. The Homalco are also known as the Mainland Comox. Their ancestral tongue is the Comox language.

Hoopa

The People of Hoopa Valley are one of California's first cultures. They traditionally occupied lands in the far northwestern corner of California. Their traditional language belongs to the Athabascan Language family and their traditional way of life was based on the semiannual king salmon runs that still occur on the Trinity River, which flows through the center of the Hoopa Valley Reservation. In addition, they made use of other indigenous foods, especially acorns. Both these resources remain important as ceremonial foods. (Source: The Official Website of the Hoopa Valley Indian Tribe - http://hoopa-nsn.gov/culture/history.htm)

Hopi

The Hopi Tribe is a sovereign Nation located in northeastern Arizona. The reservation occupies part of Coconino and Navajo counties, encompasses more than 1.5 million acres, and is made up of 12 villages on three mesas. Since time immemorial the Hopi people have lived in Hopituskwa and have maintained their sacred covenant with Maasaw, the ancient caretaker of the earth, to live as peaceful and humble farmers respectful of the land and its resources. (Source: The Official Website of the Hopi Tribe - http://hopi-nsn.gov/)

Hopland Pomo

The Hopland Band of Pomo Indians of the Hopland Rancheria is a federally recognized tribe of Pomo people in Mendocino County, California, south of Ukiah. The Hopland Band Pomos traditionally lived in the Sanel Valley.

Houma

The Houma Tribe, thought to be Muskogean-speaking like other Choctaw Tribes, was recorded living along the Red River on the east side of Mississippi River. No longer used regularly, the indigenous Houma language is thought to have fallen out of use by the late 19th century. As a result of a language shift that began during the French colonial period in Louisiana, a majority of Houma people today speak Louisiana French.

Hualapai

The Hualapai or Walapai (Hualapai: Hwalbáy) are a tribe of Native Americans who live in the mountains of northwestern Arizona, United States. The name is derived from "hwa:l," the Hualapai word for ponderosa pine, "Hualapai" meaning "people of the ponderosa pine."

Huaorani

The Huaorani, Waorani or Waodani, also known as the Waos, are native Amerindians from the Amazonian Region of Ecuador. They speak the Huaorani language, a linguistic isolate that is not known to be related to any other language. Their ancestral lands are located between the Curaray and Napo rivers. In the last 40 years, they have shifted from a hunting and gathering society to live mostly in permanent forest settlements.

Huelel (See Esselen)

Huichol

The Huichol or Wixáritari are a Native American ethnic group of western central Mexico, living in the Sierra Madre Occidental range in the Mexican states of Nayarit, Jalisco, Zacatecas, and Durango. They are best known to the larger world as the Huichol, however, they refer to themselves as Wixáritari ("the people") in their native Huichol language.

Huilliche

The Huilliche (Huillice) is an ethnic group of Chile, belonging to the Mapuche culture.

They spoke the Huillice language or Huilliche dialect of Mapudungun in historic times. Their name means 'southerners' (Mapudungun willi 'south' and che 'people'.)

Hunkpapa

The Hunkpapa are a Native American group, one of the seven council fires of the Lakota Sioux tribe. The name Húŋkpapȟa is a Sioux word meaning "Head of the Circle." They speak Lakȟóta, one of the three dialects of the Sioux language.

Hupa (See Hoopa)

Hupacasath (Also see Nuu-chah-nulth)

For thousands of years the Hupacasath people have owned, used, and occupied their traditional territory on Central Vancouver Island. The Hupacasath are comprised of three distinct tribes, the Muh-uulth-aht, Kleh-koot-aht and Cuu-ma-as-aht (Ahah-swinis). (Source: http://hupacasath.ca)

Huron (See Wyandot)

Huu-ay-aht

In Huu-ay-aht traditions, the resources of the forest, particularly the cedar tree, have special significance. Cedar wood and cedar bark both defined and surrounded the lives of Huu-ay-aht ancestors. From the time a newborn baby was swaddled in finely shredded bark and laid in a cedar cradle, to the time of death when one was wrapped in a cedar bark blanket and laid in a cedar coffin, cedar was an important part of everyday life. The Huu-ay-aht lived in cedar houses, cooked in cedar boxes, traveled in dugout cedar canoes, wore cedar bark clothes, and gathered and stored food in cedar baskets. (Source: http://huuayaht.org/?page_id=149)

Illini (Illiniwek, Illinois)

The Illinois Confederation, sometimes referred to as the Illiniwek or Illini, were a group of Native American tribes in the upper Mississippi River valley of North America. The tribes were the Kaskaskia, the Cahokia, the Peoria, the Tamaroa, Moingwena, Michigamea, Albiui, Amonokoa, Chepoussa, Chinkoa, Coiracoentanon, Espeminkia, Maroa, Matchinkoa, Michibousa, Negawichi, and Tapouara.

Inca

The Inca Empire was the largest empire in pre-Columbian America. The center of the empire was located in Cusco in modern-day Peru. The Incas used a variety of methods, from conquest to peaceful assimilation, to incorporate a large portion of western South America, centered on the Andean mountain ranges, including, besides Peru, large parts of modern Ecuador, western and south central Bolivia, northwest Argentina, north and central Chile, and southern Colombia into a state comparable to the historical empires of Eurasia. The official language of the empire was Quechua, although hundreds of local languages and dialects of Quechua were spoken. The Inca referred to their empire as Tawantinsuyu that can be translated as The Four Regions or The Four United Provinces.

Inde (See Jicarilla Apache)

Ineseño (Inezeño) (See Chumash)

Ingalik (Ingalit) (See Deg Xinag)

Innoko (See Holikachuk)

Innu

The Innu are the indigenous inhabitants of an area they refer to as Nitassinan ("Our Land"), which comprises most of the northeastern portions of the provinces of Quebec, Canada and some western portions of Labrador, Canada. Their ancestors were known to have lived on these lands as hunter-gatherers for several thousand years. Some coastal clans also practised agriculture, fished, and managed maple sugarbush. Their language, Innu-aimun or Ilnu (popularly known as Montagnais), is spoken throughout Nitassinan, with certain dialect differences.

In-SHUCK-ch

In-SHUCK-ch Nation is made of of three First Nations: Xa'xtsa, Skatin and Samahquam. Our councils began organizing as the Douglas, Skookumchuck and Samahquam Indian bands, in the early 1980s around the question of title. They saw this as the way to bring attention to the need for rebuilding our communities, improving our roads and creating and sustaining an economy – and finally, for bringing our people home. The three bands' work in the1980s, beginning with our councils, and then involving our members, in general assemblies, laid the groundwork for entering the treaty process, which we did, on Dec. 15, 1993. In fact, ours was the very first formal Statement of Intent to Negotiate a Treaty to be received by the BC Treaty Commission.

In-SHUCK-ch traditional territory includes the upper Harrison Lake and lower Lillooet River drainages, and our communities are situated within the lower Lillooet River valley. At present we number over 900, with three-quarters of our people living away from our territory. (Source: http://inshuckch.com)

Inuit

For more than four thousand years, Inuit — a founding people of what is now Canada — have occupied the Arctic land and waters from the Mackenzie Delta in the west, to the Labrador coast in the east and from the Hudson's Bay Coast, to the islands of the High Arctic. Inuit history was maintained through a long tradition of storytelling and legend.

Thule are the ancestors of today's Canadian Inuit. They lived much as Sivullirmiut did, in the same areas, following the migratory patterns of land and sea mammals. Archeological evidence shows the Thule culture had skills and technology to harvest large whales, seals, caribou, muskox, fish and birds, depending on the season and location. Before Europeans arrived, Inuit handcrafted their own tools from resources found on the land and in the animals they harvested. The Thule wandered by foot and dog team over large distances, depending on where harvests were plentiful. They lived in iglus (snow dwellings), which were often quite large. During the summer, they lived in tents (tupiqs) made of animal skins, or sod houses (qarmaqs). Everyone played an important role in the survival of the group. While men hunted for food, women made warm clothing from caribou and seal skins suitable for the harsh Arctic climate. Both men and women made the necessary tools. As soon as children were able, they began to learn adult roles. This way of life was practised for thousands of years until the arrival of European explorers, whalers, traders and, finally, settlers, who brought with them a new world and, indeed, a new way of life. (Source: https://itk.ca/about-inuit)

Inupiat (Inupiaq, Inupiatun)

The Iñupiat (plural) or Iñupiaq (singular) and Iñupiak (dual) (from iñuk 'person' - and -piaq 'real', i.e., 'real people') or formerly Inyupik, Inupik are the people of Alaska's Northwest Arctic and North Slope boroughs and the Bering Straits region. The Iñupiat were divided into two regional hunter-gatherer groups: the Taġiuġmiut (formerly Tareumiut) ("people of sea"), living on or near the north Alaska coast, and the Nunamiut ("people of land"), living in interior Alaska.

Iowa-Oto (Ioway)

The Iowa (also spelled Ioway), also known as the Báxoje, are a Native American Siouan people. Together with the Missouria and the Otoe, the Ioway are part of the Chiwere-speaking peoples, claiming the Ho-Chunks as their "grandfathers."

Iroquois (See Haudenosaunee)

Ishak (See Atakapa)

Isleño

Isleño is the Spanish word meaning "islander". The Isleños are the inhabitants of Canary Island, and by extension the descendants of Canarian settlers and immigrants to Louisiana, Cuba, Dominican Republic, Venezuela, Puerto Rico, and other parts of America. The name "islander" was given to the Canary Islanders to distinguish them from Spanish mainlanders known as "peninsulars" but in these places or countries, the name has evolved from a category to an identity.

Itza Maya (Itzah)

The Itza are a Guatemalan ethnic group of Maya affiliation speaking the Itza' language. They inhabit the Petén department of Guatemala in and around the city of Flores on the Lake Petén Itzá.

Iviatim (See Cahuilla)

Jackson Rancheria Band

The Jackson Rancheria Band of Miwuk (also see Miwok) Indians was first recognized by the Federal Government in 1898. Over 100 years later the Tribe enjoys self-sufficiency and self-reliance thanks to the vision and determination of one small Indian woman. Margaret L. (Hughes) Dalton was born in Tuolumne, California to her Native American Mother, Tessie Jeff, and her non-Indian Father, Clyde Hughes. After completing her ninth grade year at Calaveras High School, she left school and married Earl Dalton, Sr. in 1956, when she was 16 years old. Their dream was to make their small Band of Miwuk Indians self-sufficient, not dependent on any state or government funding. It was a journey that would take over 40 years to complete. (Source: http://jacksoncasino.com/tribal/history)

Jamestown S'Klallam

For ten thousand years, a Nation of people lived and prospered on the lands now known as the Olympic Peninsula in the State of Washington. These strong people of the S'Klallam Tribes had a system of governance, engaged in commerce, managed natural and human resources, and exercised power over their homelands. The S'Klallam created a rich culture of art, song, spirituality, traditional knowledge and social structure. The S'Klallam culture promoted leadership, self-sufficiency, self-reliance, and a code of conduct within their community that served as a basis for strength, pride and survival. This was a Nation, a government and a community... independent and interdependent. It still is. (Source: http://jamestowntribe.org/history/hist_jst.htm)

Jamul (Also see Kumeyaay)

The Jamul Indian Village of California is a federally recognized tribe of Kumeyaay Indians who are sometimes known as Mission Indians.

Jemez Pueblo

Jemez Pueblo is in Sandoval County, New Mexico, United States. Among Pueblo members it is known as Walatowa. Jemez (also Towa) is a Kiowa–Tanoan language spoken by the Jemez Pueblo people in New Mexico. It has no written form, as tribal rules do not allow it.

Jena Band (Choctaw)

The earliest recorded notice of the Choctaw Indians is believed to be about 1540, in the area of southern Mississippi and in the early 1700s near present-day Mobile, Alabama, Biloxi, Mississippi, and New Orleans, Louisiana. Inland from these settlements there was a large tribe of Muskogean speaking people occupying about 60 towns on the streams that formed the headwaters of the Pascagoula and Pearl Rivers. (Source: jenachoctaw.org/history.html). The Jena Band is one of three federally recognized Choctaw groups in the United States. They are based in La Salle and Catahoula Parishes in the U.S. state of Louisiana. The Jena Band received federal recognition in 1995. Tribal membership totals 241.

Jicarilla Apache

The Jicarillas were one of six southern Athapascan groups which migrated out of Canada sometime between A.D. 1300 and 1500. Their traditional American Southwest homeland covered more than 50 million acres spreading across the central and eastern region of norther New Mexico and adjoining portions of southern Colorado and western Oklahoma. The geography of this region is comprised of fundamental environments which helped shape the basic social organization of the Jicarillas into two bands: the Llaneros, or plains people, and the Olleros, or mountain-valley people. The name "Jicarilla" (pronounced hek-a-REH-ya) comes from a Spanish word generally defined as '"little basket maker" referring to a small gourd or basket. (Source: http://.jicarillaonline.com/History/jic_apachehistory.html)

Juaneño

The Juaneño or Acagchemem are an indigenous tribe of Southern California. The Juaneño lived in what is now part of Orange and San Diego Counties and received their Spanish name from the priests of the California mission chain due to their proximity to Mission San Juan Capistrano. Today they call themselves the Juaneño Band of Mission Indians, Acjachemen Nation.

Kadohadacho

The Kadohadacho are a Native American Tribe within the Caddo Confederacy. The Kadohadacho traditionally lived at the borders of Texas, Oklahoma, Arkansas, and Louisiana. They cultivated crops, such as corn, beans, squash, and pecans, and manufactured bows and pottery for trade.

Kainai

The Blood Tribe / Kainai and its confederates, the Peigan and Siksika, are considered to be the oldest residents of the western prairie region. Blackfoot is found to be so diverse from other language groups, leading linguists to believe that the Blackfoot people have lived apart from other language groups for an extended period of time. Archeologists date the existence of a plains hunting culture in the area to 11,000 years before present. The Blood Tribe was a vibrant, self reliant and self-sufficient society. Its traditional territory, rich in natural resources supplied all its basic economic needs. Its well-developed social structure, cultural and political systems provided a solid foundation that allowed excellence in every aspect of life. The Blood Tribe was allied politically, culturally, and economically with the Siksika (Blackfoot), and Peigans (North and South Peigans) forming what historians refer to as the Blackfoot Confederacy. (Source: bloodtribe.org)

Kalapuya

The Kalapuya is a Native American Tribe and are members of the Confederated Tribes of the Grand Ronde Community of Oregon. The Kalapuya Tribe's traditional homelands were the Willamette Valley of present-day western Oregon in the United States, an area bounded by the Cascade Mountains at the east and the Oregon Coast Range at the west, the Columbia River at the north to the Calapooya Mountains of the Umpqua River at the south.

Kali'na (See Carib)

Kalispel (See Pend d'Oreilles)

Kanak

Kanak (formerly also Canaque) are the indigenous Melanesian inhabitants of New Caledonia, in the southwest Pacific. Melanesia is a subregion of Oceania extending from the western end of the Pacific Ocean to the Arafura Sea, and eastward to Fiji. Though Melanesian settlement is recorded on Grande Terre's Presqu'île de Foué peninsula as far back as the Lapita culture, the origin of Kanak people is unclear.

Kanaka Maoli

The Kānaka Maoli or Hawaii Maoli refers to the indigenous Polynesian people of the Hawaiian Islands or their descendants. Native Hawaiians trace their ancestry back to the original Polynesian settlers of Hawaii.

Kanien'kehá:ka (Mohawk)

Kanien'kehá:ka ("People of the Place of Flint") are an Iroquoian-speaking indigenous people of North America originally from the Mohawk Valley in upstate New York. Their territory ranged to present-day southern Quebec and eastern Ontario. As original members of the Iroquois League, the Mohawk were known as the "Keepers of the Eastern Door", they guarded the Iroquois Confederation against invasion from that direction by Tribes from the New England and lower New York areas. Mohawk religion is predominantly Animist.

Kanza (See Kaw)

Karankawa

Karankawa (also Karankawan, Carancahua, Clamcoëhs, and Auia) were a group of Native American tribes who had a common dialect and culture. These people can be more specifically identified as the Capoques (Cocos), Kohanis, Kopanes, Kronks, and Karankawa (Carancaquacas) bands. They inhabited the Gulf Coast of Texas from Galveston Bay in the present-day Greater Houston area, south to Corpus Christi Bay.

Karen

The Karen (or Kayin people) refers to a number of Sino-Tibetan language speaking ethnic groups which reside primarily in southern and southeastern Burma (Myanmar). A large number of Karen resides in Thailand, mostly on the Thai–Burmese border.

Karkin (See Ohlone)

Karuk

Karuk (also Karok) are an indigenous people of California in the United States. They are one of the largest Tribes in California today. Since time immemorial, the Karuk, whose name means "upriver people", or "upstream" people, have resided in villages along the Klamath River, where they continue such cultural traditions as hunting, gathering, fishing, basket making and ceremonial dances. The Karuk were the only California Tribe to grow tobacco plants.

Kashaya

Kashaya (also Southwestern Pomo, Kashia) is a name for a branch of Pomo people whose historical home is the Pacific Coastline of what is now Sonoma County, California.

Kaska Dena

Kaska Dena have lived in over 240,000 square kilometres of land in the southeast Yukon, southern Northwest Territories, and north-western British Columbia for tens of thousands of years; long before both recorded history and the existence of provincial land and territorial borders. While we have always viewed ourselves as one Nation, provincial and territorial borders now separate Kaska families, and Kaska have been divided into Bands by the Indian Act. The five traditional Kaska groups are now referred to as First Nations. The Kaska First Nations in British Columbia are: the Dease River First Nation at Good Hope Lake; the Daylu Dena Council at Daylu (Lower Post); and the Kwadacha First Nation at Fort Ware, north of Prince George, BC. The Kaska First Nations in Yukon are: the Liard First Nation at Watson Lake, and the Ross River Dena Council at Ross River. (Source: http://kaskadenacouncil.com/kaska-dena/our-history)

Kaskaskia

The Kaskaskia were one of about a dozen cognate tribes that made up the Illiniwek Confederation or Illinois Confederation. Their longstanding homeland was in the Great Lakes region.

Kathlamet

The Kathlamet is a Tribe of Native American people with a historic homeland along the Columbia River in southwestern Washington state. The Kathlamet people originally spoke the Kathlamet language, a dialect of the Chinookan language.

Kato (See Cahto)

Katzie First Nation

The Katzie First Nation once comprised at least ten villages throughout the territory. The Katzie First Nation derives its name from the Halkomelem word for a type of moss, and it is also the name of an ancient village site in the immediate vicinity of the Katzie Indian Reserve at Pitt Meadows. The only other Katzie village sites permanently occupied at the time of this writing are the Katzie reserves at Barnston Island and at Yorkson Creek in Langley. The people now known as the Katzie First Nation were granted rights and title to their territory and their resources by the Creator, by Khaals, by their first Chiefs and from the reiteration of customs from time out of mind. Long before the emergence of any other human community in the Lower Fraser region, the Creator placed five communities, each with its own chief, at different locations on the Land. Those locations are now known as Pitt Lake, Sheridan Hill, Port Hammond, Point Roberts and Point Grey. (Source: http://katzie.ca/katzie_history_part_1.htm)

Kaw

The Kaw Nation (or Kanza) is a Native American Tribe in Oklahoma. They come from the central Midwestern United States. The Tribe known as Kaw has also been known as the "People of the South Wind", "People of water", also called, variously, Kansa, Kaza, Kosa, and Kasa. Their tribal language is Kansa, classified as a Siouan language. The Kaw are closely related to the Osage Nation, with whom members often intermarried.

Kawaiisu

The Kawaiisu, also "Nuwa or Nuooah", are indigenous to the remote and rural Tehachapi and Paiute Mountain areas of California's Sierra Nevada foothills. Because of relocation by the United States Government in the late 1800's, their traditions such as dress, music, songs, and knowledge of sacred sites have been mostly lost with only their language, traditional stories, and survival skills remaining. (Source: Kawaiisu Language & Cultural Center - http://kawaiisu.org/)

Kawésqar (See Alacalufe)

Kawlic (See Upper Cowlitz)

Kenaitze

Kahtnuht'ana Dena'ina people have inhabited the Kenai Peninsula since time immemorial. Today, Kenaitze Indian Tribe is federally recognized under the Indian Reorganization Act as a sovereign independent nation. Many of the Tribe's more than 1,400 members still live on the Kenai Peninsula and in Anchorage.

Kewa Pueblo

Kewa Pueblo, formerly known as Santo Domingo Pueblo (Eastern Keres: Kewa), is an Indian pueblo in Sandoval County, New Mexico. The population of the pueblo is composed of Native Americans who speak an eastern dialect of the Keresan languages. The Pueblo celebrates an annual feast day on August 4 to honor their patron saint, St. Dominic, where more than 2,000 pueblo people participate in traditional corn dances.

Kichai

The Kichai Tribe (also Keechi or Kitsai) was a Native American Southern Plains tribe that inhabited northeastern Texas. Their name for themselves was K'itaish, and they are most closely related to the Pawnee.

Kickapoo

The Kickapoo (Kiikaapoa or Kiikaapoi) are an Algonquian-speaking Native American Tribe. According to the Anishinaabeg, the name "Kickapoo" means "Stands here and there." It may have referred to the Tribe's migratory patterns. Today there are three federally recognized Kickapoo Tribes in the United States, one in Kansas, one in Oklahoma, and one in Texas.

Kilatikas (See Miami)

Kiliwa

The Kiliwa (Kiliwa: K'olew) are an Aboriginal people of northern Baja California, Mexico. Their traditional language is the Kiliwa language.

Kiowa Apache

The Kiowa are a Nation of American Indians of the Great Plains. They migrated from the western Montana into Colorado in the 17th and 18th centuries and into the Southern Plains by the 19th century. The Kiowa language is still spoken today and considered part of the Kiowa Tanoan language family.

Kispiox/Anspayaxw

Kispiox is located at the confluence of the Skeena and Kispiox Rivers. The lands of the Gitksan Nation include approximately 33,000 square kilometres in the northwest British Columbia. There are six villages within a radius of 75 kilometers in the Hazelton area. There is a distinctive dialect difference between the eastern Gitksan (Anspayaxw, Sikadok and Gitanmaax) and the western (Gitsegukla, Gitwangak and Gitanyow). The Gitksan culture, tradition and language are the basis of who we are as Gitksan. We are a matrilineal society and all members are born into their House Group and follow their mother. Our feast system is our governing body where the business is taken care of. Feasts are very much alive and practiced within the Gitksan territory. (Source: http://kispioxband.com)

Kitanemuk

The Kitanemuk are an indigenous people of California. They traditionally lived in the Tehachapi Mountains and the Antelope Valley area of the western Mojave Desert of southern California.

Kitasoo/Xai'xais

Thousands of Years of History Awaits You in the Home of the Spirit Bear. Klemtu is home to the Kitasoo/Xai'xais people. Two distinct tribal organizations live here: the Kitasoo (Tsimshian) who were originally from Kitasu Bay and the Xai'xais of Kynoc Inlet. The Kitasoo/Xai'xais people are the only permanent residents within the traditional territories of this First Nation. The Tsimshian (Tsim-she-yan, meaning "People of the Skeena) of this part of BC's Pacifc West Coast lived in small villages that were scattered along the rivers, bays, and inlets of the central coast before the major arrival of Europeans. They had created a flourishing culture and maintained their way of life for thousands of years, developing elaborate social and political hierarchical structures supported by highly organized and lavish ceremonies. (Source: http://spiritbear.com/site/our_culture/kitasoo-xai--xais_history.html)

Kitselas (See Tsimshian)

Kizh

The Kizh (Kitc) Gabrieleño Heritage (Indigenous people of the willow branch, tulle, and brush houses). Today there is a growing awareness of the enormous debt that Los Angeles owes the Gabrieleño. Although the city traditionally traces its cultural heritage to Spanish and American roots, it was the Gabrieleño who built and supported the missions, Pueblo, and ranchos. It was the Gabrieleño who provided the goods and labor that enabled the first settlements to survive and prosper; without them the history of Los Angeles would be very different indeed. From: "The First Angelinos," by William McCawley.

The Kizh (Kitc) Gabrieleños are the indigenous people of the Los Angeles basin that were enslaved to build the San Gabriel mission as well as the Los Angeles Plaza Church and who's history has attempted to be erased by politics on both local and federal levels. We are talking about a conspiracy through the 20th century to avoid the question of repatriation. (Source: gabrielenoindians.org)

Klahoose

The Klahoose is a First Nations government located on Cortes Island and surrounding Toba Inlet, in southwestern British Columbia. The Klahoose are part of, with the Sliammon, Homalco, and K'omoks, the larger grouping of the Comox people, which is a subgroup of the Coast Salish. Their ancestral tongue is the Comox language. We, the Klahoose people, are the original caretakers of the land. We live by our values which are based on our culture, tradition, unity, and equality. Our solid economy is built on holistic practice and respect for ourselves, our territory and the environment. Social well-being, good health and education are essential for a safe, prosperous community. Through our vision, the Klahoose community ensures a future for our children and the generations that follow. (Source: http://klahoose.org/about/)

Klallam

Klallam, or Clallam, (although the spelling with "K" is preferred in all four modern Klallam communities) refers to four related indigenous Native American/First Nations communities from the Pacific Northwest of North America. The Klallam culture is classified ethnographically and linguistically in the Coast Salish subgroup. The word "Klallam" comes from the North Straits Salish language name for the Klallam people.

Klamath

The Klamath are a Native American Tribe of the Plateau culture area in Southern Oregon. They lived in the area around the Upper Klamath Lake and the Klamath, Williamson, and Sprague rivers. They subsisted primarily on fish and gathered roots and seeds and were known to raid neighbouring Tribes and occasionally to take prisoners as slaves. They traded with the Chinookan people.

Klickitat

The Klickitat (also spelled Klikitat) are a Native American tribe of the Pacific Northwest. The Klickitat were noted for being active and enterprising traders, and served as intermediaries between the coastal tribes and those living east of the Cascade Mountains.

Kogi

The Kogi, or Cogui or Kágaba (translated "jaguar" in the Kogi language) are a Native American ethnic group that lives in the Sierra Nevada de Santa Marta in Colombia. Their civilization has continued since the Pre-Columbian era. The Kogi language belongs to the Chibchan family.

K'ómoks

For thousands of years indigenous people occupied the shoreline of eastern Vancouver Island in a place referred to as, "the land of plenty". This Land of Plenty stretched from what is known today as Kelsey Bay south to Hornby and Denman Island and included the watershed and estuary of the Puntledge River. The people called K'ómoks today referred to themselves as Sathloot, Sasitla, Ieeksun, Puntledge, Cha'chae, and Tat'poos. They occupied sites in Kelsey Bay, Quinsum, Campbell River, Quadra Island, Kye Bay, and along the Puntledge estuary. As a cultural collective they called themselves, "Sathloot", according to the late Mary Clifton. (Source: http://comoxband.ca/history.php)

Koorie

The Koori (from Awabakal language gurri, as spoken in the area of what is today Newcastle, adopted by indigenous people of other areas) are the indigenous Australians that traditionally occupied modern day New South Wales and Victoria. The term is used by the Aboriginal people of Victoria, parts of New South Wales and Tasmania, describing the indigenous people's own word for themselves. It was originally a word from the North-Coast of New South Wales.

Kootenai (See Flathead Salish)

Kootenay (See Ktunaxa)

Korowai

The Korowai, also called the Kolufo, are a people of southeastern Papua New Guinea. Until 1970, they were unaware of the existence of any people other than themselves. The Korowai language belongs to the Awyu–Dumut family and is part of the Trans–New Guinea phylum. The majority of the Korowai clans live in tree houses on their isolated territory.

Korubo

Korubo or Korubu is the name given to a Tribe of indigenous people living in the lower Javari Valley of the western Amazon Basin. The group calls themselves 'Dslala'. The Korubo are some of the last people on Earth to live in near isolation from modern society.

Koso (See Shoshone)

Koyukon

The Koyukon are a group of Athabaskan people living in northern Alaska. Their traditional home is along the Koyukuk and Yukon rivers where they have subsisted by hunting and trapping for thousands of years. The Koyukon language belongs to a widespread family called Na-Dene or Athabaskan.

Ktunaxa

Ktunaxa (pronounced 'k-too-nah-ha' or Kootenay in English) people have occupied the lands adjacent to the Kootenay and Columbia Rivers and the Arrow Lakes of British Columbia, Canada for more than 10,000 years. For thousands of years the Ktunaxa people enjoyed the natural bounty of the land, seasonally migrating throughout our Traditional Territory to follow vegetation and hunting cycles. (Source: Official web site of the Ktunaxa Nation Council and Ktunaxa Nation - http://ktunaxa.org/who/index.html)

Kumeyaay

The Kumeyaay, also known as Tipai-Ipai, Kamia, or formerly Diegueño, are Native American people of the extreme southwestern United States and northwest Mexico. They live in the states of California in the US and Baja California in Mexico. In Spanish, the name is commonly spelled Kumiai. The Kumeyaay consist of two related groups, the Ipai and Tipai.

Kuna

Kuna or Cuna is the name of an indigenous people of Panama and Colombia. The spelling Kuna is currently preferred. In the Kuna language, the name is Dule or Tule, meaning "people," and the name of the language in Kuna is Dulegaya, meaning "Kuna language" (literally "people-mouth").

Kwakiutl

The Kwakiutl District Council is a Political organization representing ten of the fifteen bands of the Kwakawaka'wakw (Kwakawala speaking peoples). These bands are located on the northeastern and northwestern end of Vancouver Island and the adjacent mainland between Comox Valley to the south and Smith Inlet to the north. Each of the bands has its own distinctive name but, as a result of the work of early anthropologists, these bands, as a group have come to be widely know as the Southern Kwakiutl. Because of this, the District Council has found it politically advantageous to use the term "Kwakiutl" for its name. Overall the Kwakiutl District Council, in its various capacities, represents aboriginal people in the Kwakiutl Nation. The member Nations are: Mamalilikulla Qwe'Qwa'Sot'Em First Nation, Da'naxda'xw First Nation, Cape Mudge First Nation, Campbell River First Nation, K'omoks First Nations, Kwiakah First Nation, Gwa'sala-'Nakwaxda'wx First Nation, Tlatlasikwala First Nation, Kwakiutl First Nation and Quatsino First Nation. (Source: http://kdchealth.com/)

Kwakwaka'wakw

The Kwakwaka'wakw are an Indigenous people with an approximate population of 5,500, who live in British Columbia on northern Vancouver Island and the adjoining mainland and islands. The same people were historically misnamed and identified as Kwakiutl as well. Their language, now spoken by less than 5% of the population (about 250 people), consists of four dialects of what is commonly referred to as Kwak'wala. The name Kwakwaka'wakw translates as "The-Kwak'wala-Speaking-People".

Kwanlin Dün

We are the Citizens of the Kwanlin Dün First Nation. For many generations, our people have lived along the Chu Nínkwän (today, the Yukon River). Linguistically, the Kwanlin Dün is affiliated with the Southern Tutchone Tribal Council. (Source: http://kwanlindun.com/about)

Kwantlen First Nation

The Kwantlen are Sto:lo people, or "river people" who depend upon the river and land for their survival and livelihood. The Sto:lo share a common language known a Halkomelem (Halq'eméylem), of the Coast Salish language family. Halkomelem contains three different dialect groups, which include Island, Downriver and Upriver Halkomelem. While groups in and around Chilliwack and Hope spoke upriver dialects, the Kwantlen (along with six other groups) spoke a dialect of downriver Halkomelem (Hun'qumi'num). Anthropologist Wayne Suttles noted that the downriver group had winter villages from the mouth of the Fraser to about as far as the Stave River. (Source: http://kwantlenfn.ca/html/history.html)

Kwiakah

Kwiakah First Nation are Lekwala speaking peoples. The Kwiakah are identified as part of the Laich-Kwil-Tach. The Laich-Kwil-Tach are the southernmost speakers of this northern Wakashan language. The traditional material culture, subsistence, social organization, religious and ceremonial practices of the Kwakw ak a'wakw were extensively documented in the late 19th and early 20th century by Franz Boas. At present only 20 members are registered as Kwiakah First Nations. Under the leadership of Chief Steven Dick the nation has begun to become again a major player in the Kwiakah Tratitional Territory. (Source: http://kwiakah.com/)

Kwicksutaineuk-ah-kwa-mish

The Kwicksutaineuk-ah-kwa-mish First Nation is a First Nations band government based on northern Vancouver Island in British Columbia, Canada, in the Queen Charlotte Strait region. It is a member of the Musgamagw Tsawataineuk Tribal Council, along with the 'Namgis First Nation and the Tsawataineuk First Nation. The territory of the Kwicksutaineuk-ah-kwa-mish First Nation spans the southern Broughton Archipelago and the Gilford Island area just north of the mouth of Knight Inlet. The main village of the Kwicksutaineuk-ah-kwa-mish is Gwa'yasdams, is a small community located on Gilford Island.

Laguna

The Laguna Pueblo (Western Keres: Kawaik) is a Tribe of the Pueblo people in west-central New Mexico, USA. The name, Laguna, is Spanish (meaning "lake") and derives from the lake located on their reservation. The real Keresan name of the Tribe is Kawaik and they are the largest Keresan-speaking Tribe.

Lahu

The Lahu, Ladhulsi, or Kawzhawd are an ethnic group of Southeast Asia and China. They divide themselves into a number of subgroups, such as the Lahu Na (Black Lahu), Lahu Nyi (Red Lahu), Lahu Hpu (White Lahu), Lahu Shi (Yellow Lahu) and the Lahu Shehleh. These names refer to the traditional color of the dress of each group. These do not function as Tribes or clans - there are no kin groups above that of the family.

Lake Babine Nation

Lake Babine Nation (also Nataotin, Nat'oot'en Nation) is a Babine First Nation originally based around Babine Lake. Its main community has been in Woyenne, near Burns Lake, since many of the Nation's members moved there in the 1940s.

Lakota

The Lakota people also known as Teton, Titunwan ("prairie dwellers"), or Teton Sioux ("snake, or enemy") are an indigenous people of the Great Plains. They are part of a confederation of seven related Sioux Tribes, the Očhéthi Šakówiŋ or seven council fires, and speak Lakota, one of the three major dialects of the Sioux language. The Lakota are the westernmost of the three Siouan language groups, occupying lands in both North and South Dakota.

Lassik (See Eel River)

Lawa

Lawa, Lawi, or Lahwi are an ethnic group in Laos and northern Thailand. Today many Lawa still live a traditional way of life, often professing animism. They are known for extraordinary craft skills. Their language is related to that of Blang in China and Va in China and Burma and belongs to the Austroasiatic language group.

Lax Kw'alaams

Lax Kw'alaams is a jewel on the edge of the mystical coastal temperate rain forest on the northwestern coast of British Columbia. From time immemorial the Tsimshian, an adventurous sea-faring people, have lived in their traditional territories near the city of Prince Rupert. Akin to other people of the Northwest Coast, the Tsimshian were fearsome warriors living in complex cultural tapestry. It was the first Aboriginal community in B.C to officially change its English name to its Aboriginal name--from Port Simpson to Lax Kw'alaams. (Source: http:// laxkwalaams.ca /)

Lemhi Shoshone

The Lemhi Shoshone are a band of Northern Shoshone, called the Akaitikka, Agaideka, or "Eaters of Salmon." They traditionally lived in the Lemhi River Valley and along the upper Salmon River in Idaho. Bands were very fluid and nomadic, and they often interacted with and inter-married other bands of Shoshone and other Tribes, such as the Bannock.

Lenape

The Lenape are Native American people in Canada and the United States. They are also called Delaware Indians after their historic territory along the Delaware River. As a result of disruption following the American Revolutionary War and later Indian removals from the eastern United States, the main groups now live in Ontario (Canada), Wisconsin, and Oklahoma.

Lenca

The Lenca are an indigenous people of southwestern Honduras and eastern El Salvador. They once spoke the Lenca language, which is now extinct. In Honduras, the Lenca are the largest indigenous group. The pre-Conquest Lenca had frequent contact with various Maya groups as well as other indigenous peoples of Mexico and Central America. Some scholars have suggested that the Lenca were not originally indigenous to Mesoamerica region, but migrated there from South America around 3,000 years ago.

Lenni-Lenape (See Lenape)

Lil'wat (Also see St'at'imc)

Today, Lil'wat traditional ways of life continue to be important within our local economy here in the northwest of British Columbia, Canada. Fish, game, plant foods and medicines are still harvested and prepared in the traditional manner are bought and traded with neighbouring First Nations.

Traditional crafts remain important both economically and culturally. The Lil'wat people are famous for our intricate basketry with patterns created from cedar roots, cedar bark, wild cherry bark and various grasses and reeds. Hand drums made from wood and the skins of deer, coyote, and moose created by skilled artisans are highly sought after, as are the detailed cedar carvings of both functional and decorative items.

The Lil'wat Nation continues to assert its right to manage the resources of our land. For clearly, our culture and livelihood depend upon a healthy environment and access to it. Through dedication, perseverance and innovative partnerships we are maintaining our traditional stewardship of the land in contemporary ways. (Source: http://lilwat.ca/)

Lipan Apache

Lipan Apache are Southern Athabascan (Apachean) people whose traditional te ritory includes present-day Texas, New Mexico, Colorado and the northern Mex can states of Chihuahua, Nuevo León, Coahuila, and Tamaulipas. Present-day Lipans mostly live throughout the U.S. Southwest, in Texas, New Mexico and the San Carlos Apache Indian Reservation in Arizona, as well as with the Mescalero tribe on the Mescalero Reservation in New Mexico.

Listiguj (Listuguj)

The Listuguj Mi'gmaq First Nation is a Canadian community. The community is allied to other Mi'gmaq communities in the Gaspé region of Quebec and in northern New Brunswick. Together, their elected Chiefs advance ancestral claims to self-government and to the traditional territory called Gespe'gewa'gi ('Kespékewáki), the last land.

Lisu

The Lisu people are a Tibeto-Burman ethnic group who inhabit the mountainous regions of Burma (Myanmar), Southwest China, Thailand, and the Indian state of Arunachal Pradesh. The Lisu form one of the 56 ethnic groups officially recognized by the People's Republic of China. In Burma, the Lisu are known as one of the seven Kachin minority groups. Approximately 55,000 live in Thailand, where they are one of the six main hill Tribes.

Lnuk (L'nuk, L'nu'k, Lnu) (See Mi'kmaq)

Lokono (See Arawak)

Loucheux (Loucheaux) (See Gwich'in)

Loup (See Nipmuc)

Lower Chehlais (See Chehalis Tribe)

Lower Coquille (See Coquille)

Lower Cowlitz (See Cowlitz)

Lower Umpqua (See Umpqua)

Lubicon

The Lubicon Lake Indian Nation is a Cree First Nation in Northern Alberta, Canada. They are commonly referred to as the Lubicon Lake Nation, Lubicon Cree or the Lubicon Lake Cree. The Nation has been embroiled with the Government of Canada regarding disputed land claims for decades. Their primary complaint is that oil and gas development on or near their land has dangerously threatened their way of life, their culture, and the health of those in their community.

Luckiamute (Lukiamute) (See Kalapuya)

Luiseño

The Luiseño, or Payomkowishum, are a Native American people who at the time of the first contacts with the Spanish in the 16th century inhabited the coastal area of southern California, ranging from Los Angeles County to San Diego County. In the Luiseño language, the people call themselves Payomkowishum (also spelled Payom-kawichum), meaning "People of the West."

Lumbee

The Lumbee Tribe is the largest Tribe in North Carolina, the largest Tribe east of the

Mississippi River and the ninth largest in the nation. The Lumbee take their name from the Lumbee River which winds its way through Robeson County. Pembroke, North Carolina is the economic, cultural and political center of the Tribe. The ancestors of the Lumbee were mainly Cheraw and related Siouan-speaking Tribes. (Source: http://lumbeeTribe.com/index.php?option=com_content&view=artic le&id=135&Itemid=115)

Lummi

The Lummi, also known as Lhaq'temish, governed by the Lummi Nation, are a Na-tive American Tribe of the Coast Salish ethnolinguistic group in western Washington state in the United States. The traditional lifestyle of the Lummi, like many Northwest Coast Tribes, consisted of the collecting of shellfish, the gathering of plants such as Camas and different species of berries, and most importantly the fishing of salmon.

Lytton First Nation

Lytton First Nation is located on 14,161 acres of land divided into 56 reserves. The re-serves are located at the site of the Indian Village of Kumsheen, meaning, "where the Rivers Cross". The Lytton First Nation is rich in natural resources. Water availability is perhaps one of the most significant natural resources available to the Nation. The Stein River water system meets the water needs of a large proportion of community members while other community wells provide water to other members. Natural spring waters are available in various areas. (Source: http://lyttonfirstnations.ca)

Maasai

The Maasai people of East Africa live in southern Kenya and northern Tanzania along the Great Rift Valley on semi-arid and arid lands. The Maasai live in Kraals arranged in a circular fashion. The fence around the kraal is made of acacia thorns, which pre-vent lions from attacking the cattle. Traditionally, kraals are shared by an extended family. Tradion has it that lions walk around the Maasai for to this day young boys can earn their adulthood by their success in a lion hunt – with a spear, not a gun.

Macushi (Macusi, Makushi)

The Macushi (Portuguese: Macuxi) are an indigenous people living in the border-lands of southern Guyana, northern Brazil in the province of Roraima, and the eastern of Venezuela. The Macushi are also known as the Macusi, Macussi, Makushi, Makusi, Makuxi, Teueia, and Teweya people. They speak the Macushi language, a Macushi-Kapon language, which is part of the Carib language family.

Mahican (See Kanien'kehá:ka)

Maidu

The Maidu are an indigenous people of northern California. They reside in the central Sierra Nevada, in the drainage area of the Feather and American Rivers. In Maiduan languages, Maidu means "Man." There are three subcategories of Maidu: Southern Maidu, Mountain Maidu, and Konkow (Koyom'kawi/Concow).

Makah

Bordered by the Strait of Juan de Fuca and the Pacific Ocean, pre-contact Makah held a vast area of inland and coastal territory. The Makah skillfully utilized the bounty of the sea. From seals to salmon to whales, the sea was - and still is - a large part of the livelihood of the Makah. (Source: http://makah.com/history.html)

Malahat (MÁLEXEŁ) (See W̱SÁNEĆ)

MÁLEXEŁ (Malahat) (See W̱SÁNEĆ)

Maliseet (Maliceet, Malisit, Malisset)

The Wolastoqiyik, or Maliseet, are an Algonquian-speaking Native American/First Nations/Aboriginal people of the Wabanaki Confederacy. They are the Indigenous people of the Saint John River valley and its tributaries, crossing the borders of New Brunswick and Quebec in Canada, and Maine in the United States.

Mandan

The Mandan are a Native American people living in North Dakota. Historically they lived along the banks of the Missouri River and two of its tributaries—the Heart and Knife Rivers—in present-day North and South Dakota. Speakers of Mandan, a Siouan language, the people developed a settled culture in contrast to that of more nomadic Tribes in the Great Plains region. There is an old myth that the Mandan had contact with early Welsh travelers (pre-Columbus) but this is generally considered to be just that – a myth.

Manobo

The Manobo are probably the most numerous of the ethnic groups of the Philippines in terms of the relationships and names of the various groups that belong to this fam-ily of languages. The groups occupy such a wide area of distribution that localized groups have assumed the character of distinctiveness as a separate ethnic grouping such as the Bagobo or the Higaonon, and the Atta.

Māori

The Māori are the indigenous Polynesian people of New Zealand. The Māori originated with settlers from eastern Polynesia. The Polynesian settlers developed a unique culture that became known as the "Māori", with their own language, a rich mythology, distinctive crafts and performing arts. Early Māori formed tribal groups, based on eastern Polynesian social customs and organization. Horticulture flourished using plants they introduced, and later a prominent warrior culture emerged.

Mapuche (Mapudungun, Mapudugan)

The Mapuche are a group of indigenous inhabitants of south-central Chile and southwestern Argentina. They constitute a wide-ranging ethnicity composed of vari-ous groups who shared a common social, religious and economic structure, as well as a common linguistic heritage. At the time of the Spanish arrival the Araucanian Mapuche inhabited the valleys between the Itata and Toltén rivers, The Huilliche and the Cuncos lived as far south as the Chilean Archipelago.

Maricopa

The Maricopa or Piipaash, are a Native American tribe, who live in the Salt River Pima-Maricopa Indian Community and Gila River Indian Community. The Maricopa are a River Yuman group, formerly living along the banks of the Colorado River.

Massachusett (Massachusetts)

The Massachusett is a tribe of Native Americans who historically lived in areas sur-rounding Massachusetts Bay in what is now the Commonwealth of Massachusetts, in particular present-day Greater Boston. Tribal members spoke the Massachusett language, part of the Algonquian family. The present-day U.S state Massachusetts is named after the tribe.

Massasoit (Massassoit, Mashpee) (See Wampanoag)

Matawa

Matawa First Nations is a Tribal Council of nine Northern Ontario First Nations lo-cated in Nishnawbe Aski Nation (NAN). The people of Matawa First Nations believe in putting community needs first. They are committed to supporting each other and working together as a regional group in order to build community strength for the future. (Source: http://matawa.on.ca)

Matlatzinca

Matlatzinca is a name used to refer to different indigenous ethnic groups in the Toluca Valley in the state of México, located in the central highlands of Mexico. The term is applied to the ethnic group inhabiting the valley of Toluca and to their language, Mat-latzinca. When used as an ethnonym, Matlatzinca refers to the people of Matlatzinco. Matlatzinco was the Aztec (Nahuatl) term for the Toluca Valley.

Mattabesset

Mattabesset or Mattabeseck refers to the Native American group which had its principal settlement at the Mattabeseck River of what is today Connecticut, United States. It is presumed that the portage offered the Mattabeseck additional opportuni-ties for trade. The Mattabeseck River also forms an extensive swampland where it meets the Connecticut, which would also have offered a variety of natural resources for exploitation.

Mattaponi

The Mattaponi Tribe is one of only two Virginia Indian Tribes in the Commonwealth of Virginia that owns reservation land. The Mattaponi were one of six Tribes inherited by Chief Powhatan in the late 16th century. The Tribe spoke an Algonquian language, like other members of the Powhatan Chiefdom.

Mattole

The Mattole are a group of Native Americans traditionally living on the Mattole and Bear rivers in the vicinity of Cape Mendocino, California. A notable difference between the Mattole and other indigenous people of northwest California is that the men traditionally had facial tattoos (on the forehead), while other local groups tradi-tionally restricted facial tattooing to women. The Mattole spoke the Mattole language, an Athapaskan language that may have been closely related to that of their Eel River neighbours to the east.

Maumee (See Miami)

Maya

The Maya people constitute a diverse range of the Native American people of southern Mexico and northern Central America. The overarching term "Maya" is a collective designation to include the peoples of the region who share some degree of cultural and linguistic heritage; however, the term embraces many distinct populations, societies, and ethnic groups, who each have their own particular traditions, cultures, and historical identity.

Mayo

The Mayo are a Mexican indigenous people living in the states of Sonora and Sinaloa, originally living near the Mayo River in Sonora. In their own language they call themselves Yoreme. The Mayo language is a Uto-Aztecan language closely related to Yaqui.

Mdewkanton

Mdewakantonwan (Bdewákhathuŋwaŋ or M'DAY-wah-kahn-tahn) are one of the sub-tribes of the Isanti (Santee) Dakota (Sioux). Their historic home is Mille Lacs Lake in central Minnesota, which in the Dakota language was called mde wakan (mystic/spiritual lake). Together with the Wahpekute (Waꞏpékhute - "Shooters Among the Trees"), they form the so-called Upper Council of the Dakota or Santee Sioux (Isáŋyáthi - "Knife Makers").

Mechoopda

The Mechoopda are a Tribe of Maidu people, indigenous peoples of California. They are enrolled in the Mechoopda Indian Tribe of Chico Rancheria, a federally recognized Tribe. Historically, the Tribe has spoken Konkow, a language related to Maidu language.

Mengwe (See Iroquois)

Menominee (Menomini)

The Menominee (also spelled Menomini in early scholarly literature; known as Mamaceqtaw, "the people," in their own language and referred to as the Malominese in some historical accounts) are a Nation of Native Americans living in Wisconsin. The Menominee are part of the Algonquian-language family of North America, of which several Tribes were located around the Great Lakes.

Meskwaki (Mesquakie)

The Meskwaki (sometimes spelled Mesquakie or Meskwahki) are a Native American people often known to outsiders as the Fox tribe. They have often been closely linked to the Sauk people. In their own language, the Meskwaki call themselves Meshkwahkihaki, which means "the Red-Earths." Historically their homelands were in the Great Lakes region.

Métis

The advent of the fur trade in west central North America during the 18th century was accompanied by a growing number of mixed offspring of Indian women and European fur traders . As this population established distinct communities separate from those of Indians and Europeans and married among themselves, a new Aboriginal people emerged - the Métis people – with their own unique culture, traditions, language (Michif), way of life, collective consciousness and nationhood.

Distinct Métis communities developed along the routes of the fur trade and across the Northwest within the Métis Nation Homeland. This Homeland includes the three Prairie provinces (Manitoba, Saskatchewan, Alberta), as well as, parts of Ontario, British Columbia, the Northwest Territories and the Northern United States. Today, many of these historic Métis communities continue to exist along rivers and lakes where forts and posts were hubs of fur trade activity from Ontario westward. As well, large numbers of Métis citizens now live in urban centres within the Métis Nation Homeland; however, even within these larger populations, well-defined Métis communities exist. (Source: http://metisnation.ca/index.php/who-are-the-metis).

Louis David Riel (22 October 1844 – 16 November 1885) was a Canadian politician, a founder of the province of Manitoba, and a political and spiritual leader of the Métis people of the Canadian prairies. He led two resistance movements against the Canadian government and its first post-Confederation prime minister, Sir John A. Macdonald. Riel sought to preserve Métis rights and culture as their homelands in the Northwest came progressively under the Canadian sphere of influence. He is regarded by many today as a Canadian folk hero.

Metlakatla

Metlakatla First Nation British Columbia, is a small community that is one of the seven Tsimshian village communities in British Columbia, Canada. It is situated at Metlakatla Pass near Prince Rupert, British Columbia. It is the one Tsimshian village in Canada that is not associated with one particular tribe or set of tribes out of the Tsimshian nation's 14 constituent tribes. The name Metlakatla derives from the Tsimshian Maaxłakxaała, which means "saltwater pass." Traditionally, this site has been the collective winter village of the "Nine Tribes" of the lower Skeena River, which since 1834 have been mostly based at Lax Kw'alaams, B.C.

Miami-Illinois

The Miami are a Native American Nation originally found in what is now Indiana, southwest Michigan, and western Ohio. The name Miami derives from the Tribe's autonym (name for themselves) in their Algonquian language, Miami-Illinois, Myaamia (plural Myaamiaki); this appears to have come from an older term meaning "downstream people."

Miccosukee

The Miccosukee Tribe of Indians of Florida is a federally recognized Native American tribe in the U.S. state of Florida. They were part of the Seminole Nation until the mid-20th century, when they organized as an independent tribe, receiving federal recognition in 1962. The Miccosukee speak the Mikasuki language.

Migueleño (See Salinan)

Mi'kmaq (Mikmawisink)

The Mi'kmaq are a First Nations people, indigenous to Canada's Maritime Provinces and the Gaspé Peninsula of Quebec. They call this region Mi'kma'kik. Others today live in Newfoundland and the northeastern region of Maine. They speak the Míkmaq language. Once written in Míkmaq hieroglyphic writing, it is now written using most letters of the standard Latin alphabet. Micmac is the anglisized pronounciation of Mi'kmaq.

Author's Note: My mother, Virginia (Doyle) MacLean, an army nurse who served in Europe during WWII, knew many natural herbal remedies that she learned from her mother and grandmother in rural Nova Scotia. My mother told us that her grandmother was adopted by the Mi'kmaq in recognition of her work as a herbalist and healer.

Mingo

The Mingo are an Iroquoian group of Native Americans made up of peoples who migrated west to the Ohio Country in the mid-eighteenth century. Anglo-Americans called these migrants mingos, a corruption of mingwe, an Eastern Algonquian name for Iroquoian-language groups in general. Mingos have also been called "Ohio Iroquois" and "Ohio Seneca."

Miniconjou

The Miniconjou are a Native American people constituting a subdivision of the Lakota Sioux, who formerly inhabited an area in western South Dakota.

Minqua (See Susquehannock)

Minsi (See Lenni Lenape)

Miskitu (Mosquito)

The Miskitu are a Native American ethnic group in Central America, of whom many are mixed race. In the northern end of their territory, the people are primarily of African-Native American ancestry. Their territory extends from Cape Camarón, Honduras, to Rio Grande, Nicaragua along the Mosquito Coast, in the Western Caribbean Zone.

Mississauga

The Mississauga are a subtribe of the Anishinaabe-speaking First Nations people located in southern Ontario, Canada. They are closely related to the Ojibwa. The name "Mississauga" comes from the Anishinaabe word Misizaagiing, meaning "[Those at the] Great River-mouth."

Mississinewas (See Miami)

Mississipian

The Mississippian culture was a mound-building Native American culture that flourished in what is now the Midwestern, Eastern, and Southeastern United States from approximately 800 CE to 1500 CE, varying regionally.

One of the most visible traits of the Mississippian tradition are their immense, flat-topped "pyramids, " or earthen platform mounds. Some were terraced, or had graded roadways leading to their summits where the society's temples and the houses of their rulers once stood. Some of these mounds are truly gigantic. For example, Monk's Mound at Cahokia rises in four terraces to a height of 100 feet, its base covers 16 acres, and it contains an estimated 22 million cubic feet of earth, making it the largest earthwork ever constructed in the Americas -- perhaps in the world. Some Mississippian cities were surrounded by extensive wooden palisades. For example, at Cahokia the downtown area was surrounded by a palisade that stood 12 - 15 feet high, required 15,000 logs, and was more than 2 miles long. (Source: http://cabrillo.edu/~crsmith/mississ.html)

Missouria

The Missouria or Missouri (in their own language, Niúachi, also spelled Niutachi) are a Native American tribe that originated in the Great Lakes region of United States before European contact. The tribe belongs to the Chiwere division of the Siouan language family, together with the Iowa and Otoe. In their own language, the Missouri call themselves Niúachi, also spelled Niutachi, meaning "People of the River Mouth."

Miwok (Miwuk) (Also See Jackson Rancheria Band)

Miwok (also spelled Miwuk, Mi-Wuk, or Me-Wuk) can refer to any one of four linguistically related groups of Native Americans, indigenous to Northern California, who traditionally spoke one of the Miwokan languages in the Utian family. The word Miwok means people in their native language.

Mixe

The Mixe or Mije is an indigenous group inhabiting the eastern highlands of the Mexican state of Oaxaca. They speak the Mixe languages which are classified in the Mixe–Zoque family. The Mixe name for themselves is ayuujkjä'äy meaning "people who speak the mountain language."

Mixtec (Mixteco, Mixteca)

The Mixtec, or Mixtecos are indigenous Mesoamerican peoples inhabiting the region known as La Mixteca that covers parts of the Mexican states of Oaxaca, Guerrero and Puebla. The Mixtec region and the Miextec peoples are traditionally divided into highland Mixtecs or mixteca alta, Lowland Mixtecs or mixteca baja, and Coastal Mixtecs. The Mixtecan languages form a major branch of the Otomanguean language family.

Mlabri

The Mlabri or Mrabri are an ethnic group of Thailand and Laos. A hill Tribe in northern Thailand along the border with Laos, they have been groups of nomadic hunter-gatherers. The name Mlabri is a Thai/Lao alteration of the word Mrabri that appears to come from a Khmuic term "people of the forest". They are also known locally as Phi Tong Luang or "spirits of the yellow leaves", apparently because they abandon their shelters when the leaves begin to turn yellow.

Modoc

The Modoc are a Native American people who originally lived in the area that is now northeastern California and central Southern Oregon. They are currently divided between Oregon and Oklahoma and are enrolled in either of two federally recognized tribes, the Klamath Tribes in Oregon and the Modoc Tribe of Oklahoma.

Mohave (Mojave)

Mohave or Mojave (Mojave: 'Aha Makhav) are a Native American people indigenous to the Colorado River in the Mojave Desert. The Fort Mojave Indian Reservation includes parts of California, Arizona, and Nevada. The Colorado River Indian Reservation includes parts of California and Arizona and is shared by members of the Chemehuevi, Hopi, and Navajo peoples.

Mohawk (See Kanien'kehá:ka)

Mohegan

(Not to be confused with the Mahican or Mohawk, different Native American tribes.) The Mohegan Indian Tribe is a federally recognized tribe living on a reservation in the eastern upper Thames River valley of south-central Connecticut. It is one of two federally recognized tribes in the state, the other is The Mashantucket Pequot. There are also three state-recognized tribes. At the time of European contact, the Mohegan and Pequot were a unified tribal entity living in the lower Connecticut region, but the Mohegan gradually became independent. They were under Pequot rule briefly in the 1630s until European colonists defeated the Pequot in 1637 during the Pequot War. Under the leadership of Uncas, a sachem, the Mohegan became a separate tribe before the turn of the 18th century. Uncas' name is meant to be Wonkus, which translates to fox.

Mohican (See Kanien'kehá:ka)

Mojave (See Mohave)

Molala

The Molala (also Molale, Molalla, Molele) were a people of the Plateau culture area in central Oregon, United States. They are one of the Confederated Tribes of the Grand Ronde Community of Oregon. The Molalla language was a member of the Plateau Penutian family. It was previously considered a language isolate but is now extinct.

Monacan

The Monacan is one of several Native American Tribes recognized by the Commonwealth of Virginia in the United States. The Monacan Tribe has not been recognized as an Indian Tribe by the federal government. They are located primarily in Amherst County, Virginia near Lynchburg, Virginia. There are satellite groups in West Virginia, Maryland, and Ohio.

Monache (Mono)

The Mono are a Native American people who traditionally live in the central Sierra Nevada Mountains, the Eastern Sierra, the Mono Basin, and adjacent areas of the Great Basin. Throughout recorded history, the Mono have also been known as "Mona," "Monache," or "Northfork Mono." They are divided into the Eastern Mono and the Western Mono, roughly based on the Sierra crest.

Montaukett

The Montaukett or Montauk people are a Native American Tribe of Algonquian-speaking people from the eastern end of Long Island, New York. They are related in language as well to Native American Tribes who lived across Long Island Sound in what is now Connecticut and Rhode Island. Native relics and ruins are still visible at Theodore Roosevelt County Park, just east of the village of Montauk, New York.

Mosopelea

The Mosopelea, or Ofo, were a Native American tribe who historically inhabited the upper Ohio River. In reaction to Iroquois invasions, they moved south to the lower Mississippi River, finally settling in Louisiana and assimilating with the Siouan-speaking Biloxi and the Tunica people. They are generally classified with the speakers of the Siouan Ofo language.

Multnomah

The Multnomah were a tribe of Chinookan people who lived in the area of Portland, Oregon, more specifically Sauvie Island. Multnomah villages were located throughout the Portland basin and on both sides of the Columbia River. The Multnomah spoke a dialect of the Upper Chinookan language in the Oregon Penutian family.

Munsee (Munsie, Muncey, Muncie)

The Munsee are a subtribe of the Lenape, originally constituting one of the three great divisions of that tribe and dwelling along the upper portion of the Delaware River, the Minisink, and the adjacent county in New York, New Jersey, and Pennsylvania. From their principal totem they were frequently called the Wolf tribe of the Lenape. They were prominent in the early history of New York and New Jersey, being among the first tribes of that region to meet the European immigrants.

Muscogee (Muscogee, Muskoke)

The Muscogee (Creek) people are descendents of a remarkable culture that, before 1500 AD, spanned Alabama, Georgia, Florida and South Carolina. Early ancestors of the Muscogee constructed magnificent earthen pyramids along the rivers of this region as part of their elaborate ceremonial complexes and built expansive towns. The Muscogee were not one Tribe but a union of several which evolved into a confederacy that was the most sophisticated political organization north of Mexico. (Source: Muscogee (Creek) Nation Official Tribal Website - http://muscogeenation-nsn.gov/index.php/creek-history)

Musqueam

The Musqueam people have lived in our present location for thousands of years. Our traditional territory occupies what is now Vancouver and surrounding areas. The name Musqueam relates back to the River Grass, the name of the grass is məθkʷəy̓. We are traditional hən̓q̓əmin̓əm̓ speaking people and have descended from the cultural group known as the Coast Salish. Our people moved throughout our traditional territory using the resources the land provided for fishing, hunting, trapping and gathering, to maintain our livelihood. Today, the Musqueam people still use these resources for economical and traditional purposes. (Source: http://musqueam.bc.ca/)

Nadot'en (Natoot'en, Natut'en) (See Lake Babine Nation)

Nadouessioux

The Nadouessioux (Sioux) are a Native American and First Nations people in North

America. The term can refer to any ethnic group within the Great Sioux Nation or any of the Nation's many language dialects. The Sioux comprise three major divisions based on Siouan dialect and subculture: Isáŋyathi or Isáŋathi ("Knife,"), residing in the extreme east of the Dakotas, Minnesota and northern Iowa, often referred to as the Santee or Eastern Dakota; Iháŋkthuŋwaŋ and Iháŋkthuŋwaŋna ("Village-at-the-end" and "little village-at-the-end"), residing in the Minnesota River area. They are considered to be the middle Sioux, and are often referred to as the Yankton and the Yanktonai, or, collectively, as the Wičhíyena (endonym) or the Western Dakota; Thítȟuŋwaŋ or Teton (uncertain, perhaps "Dwellers on the Prairie"; this name is archaic among the natives, who prefer to call themselves Lakȟóta), the westernmost Sioux, known for their hunting and warrior culture. The name "Sioux" is an abbreviated form of Nadouessioux borrowed into Canadian French from Nadoüessioüak from the early Odawa exonym: naadowesiwag "Sioux."

Naga

The term Naga people refers to a conglomeration of several Tribes inhabiting the North Eastern part of India and north-western Burma. The Tribes have similar cultures and traditions, and form the majority ethnic group in the Indian states of Nagaland, Manipur, Arunachal Pradesh and Assam. The Naga speak various languages belonging to the Angami–Pochuri, Ao, Kukish, Sal, Tangkhul, and Zeme branches of Tibeto-Burman.

Nahane (Nahani, Nahanne)

Nahani (Nahane, Nahanni) is an Athapaskan word used to designate native groups located in British Columbia, Northwest Territories and the Yukon Territories between the upper Liard River and the 64th parallel north latitude. While these native groups do not necessarily have anything in common, the Canadian government used the term "Nahani" until the 1970s to refer to them collectively.

Nahua

Nahuas are a group of indigenous peoples of Mexico and El Salvador. Their language of Uto-Aztecan affiliation is called Nahuatl and consists of many more dialects and variants, a number of which are mutually unintelligible. About 1,500,000 Nahua speak Nahuatl and another 1,000,000 speak only Spanish. Evidence suggests the Nahua peoples originated in the southwestern part of what is now the United States and northwestern Mexico.

Nakoda (Nakota)

Nakoda is the endonym used by the native peoples of North America who usually go by the name of Assiniboine (or Hohe), in the United States, and of Stoney, in Canada. The Nakoda are a Siouan Native American/First Nations people originally from the Northern Great Plains of the United States and Canada. In modern times, they have been based in present-day Saskatchewan; they have also populated parts of Alberta, southwestern Manitoba, northern Montana and western North Dakota.

Nambe Pueblo

Nambé Oweenge Pueblo is a pueblo in Santa Fe County, New Mexico, United States. Nambé was one of the Pueblos that organized and participated in the Pueblo Revolt of 1680.

'Namgis

Long before the first Europeans set foot on the shores of what is now known as the Northwest Coast of British Columbia, the Kwakwaka 'wakw practiced an age-old tradition of potlatching. Extended families occupied the four corners of the Gukwdzi (Bighouse), and when it came time to commemorate a milestone in the family, the aforementioned areas were cleared away, people were invited to act as witnesses to validate the transactions, and the potlatch got underway, with the host's family performing the dances. After the arrival of the Europeans the Kwakwaka 'wakw eventually adopted the european style of housing, more through coercion for the sake of practicality than logical, rational choice. And with more and more families adopting and adapting to the european way of doing things, the place to perform ceremony and ritual had to change as well. (Source: http://namgis.bc.ca/Pages/Bighouse.aspx)

Nanticoke (See Nentego)

Nantucket (See Wampanoag)

Narragansett

The Narragansett Tribe are an Algonquian Native American Tribe from Rhode Island. The Tribe is led by an elected tribal council, a chief sachem, a medicine man, and a Christian leader. The word "Narragansett" means, literally, "People of the Small Point." Traditionally the Tribe spoke the Narragansett language, a member of the Algonquian language family.

Naskapi

The Naskapi are the indigenous Innu inhabitants of an area referred to by many Innu to as Nitassinan, which comprises most of what other Canadians refer to as eastern Quebec and Labrador, Canada. The Naskapi themselves use a different word in their language to refer to this land, st'aschinuw. Innu people are frequently divided into two groups, the Montagnais who live along the north shore of the Gulf of Saint Lawrence, in Quebec, and the less numerous Naskapi who live farther north.

Natchez

The Natchez are a Native American people who originally lived in the Natchez Bluffs area, near the present-day city of Natchez, Mississippi. They spoke a language isolate that has no known close relatives, although it may be very distantly related to the Muskogean languages of the Creek Confederacy. The Natchez are noted for being the only Mississippian culture with complex chiefdom characteristics to have survived long into the period after the European colonization of America began.

Navajo (Navaho)

The Navajo Nation extends into the states of Utah , Arizona and New Mexico , covering over 27,000 square miles of unparalleled beauty. Diné Bikéyah, or Navajoland, is larger than 10 of the 50 states in America. Visitors from around the world are intrigued and mystified when they hear the Navajo language – so, too, were the enemy during World War II. Unknown to many, the Navajo language was used to create a secret code to battle the Japanese. Navajo men were selected to create codes and serve on the front line to overcome and deceive those on the other side of the battlefield. Today, these men are recognized as the famous Navajo Code Talkers, who exemplify the unequaled bravery and patriotism of the Navajo people. (Source: http://navajo-nsn.gov/history.htm)

Nawat (See Pipil)

Nde (See Tinde)

Nee-me-poo

The Nee-me-poo (Nez Perce) are Native American people who live in the Pacific Northwest region (Columbia River Plateau) of the United States. The Nez Perce's name for themselves is Nimíipuu meaning, "The People." They speak the Nez Perce language or Niimiipuutímt, a Sahaptian language.

Nehiyaw (Nehiyawok) (See Cree)

Nentego

The Nanticoke Lenni-Lenape Indian Tribe (headquartered in Bridgeton, New Jersey) and the Lenape Indian Tribe of Delaware (headquartered in Cheswold, Delaware) have formed an intertribal union, "The Confederation of Sovereign Nentego — Lenape Tribes." The purpose of the new confederation is to promote the common good of our people, to defend our right to govern ourselves under our own laws, to protect and maintain our tribal culture and preserve the legacy of our ancestors. The confederation is an expression of the sovereignty given by the Creator to our tribal communities, a sovereignty that has continued from ancient times to the present. It is also an affirmation of the shared history and common ancestry between our interrelated tribal communities, made up of Lenape and Nanticoke (originally, "Nentego") families, which have remained in the area of their ancient homeland. (Source: nanticoke-lenape.info/confederation.htm)

Neusiok

Neusiok are an unclassified tribe, perhaps of Iroquoian stock, found in 1584 occupying the country on the south side of lower Neuse River, within the present Craven and Carteret Counties, North Carolina. They were at war with the more southerly coast tribes. In the later colonial period the people of the same region were commonly known as the Neuse and had dwindled by the year 1700 to 15 warriors in two towns, Chattooka and Rouconk. They probably disappeared by incorporation with the Tuscarora. (Source: accessgenealogy.com/native/tribes/neusiokhist.htm)

Neutrals (See Attawandaron)

Newe

The Western Shoshone call themselves Newe, "The People," and they refer to their ancestral lands as Newe Sogobia. The Western Shoshone are the most bombed nation on Earth, with over 1,000 nuclear bombs detonated on their lands by the U.S. and Great Britain. (Source: http://h-o-m-e.org/nuclear-colonialism/western-shoshone.html)

Nez Perce (See Nee-me-poo)

Ngarrindjeri

The Ngarrindjeri (literal meaning The people who belong to this land) are a Nation of eighteen "Tribes" (lakinyeri) consisting of numerous family clans who speak similar dialects of the Ngarrindjeri language and are the traditional Aboriginal people of the lower Murray River, western Fleurieu Peninsula, and the Coorong of southern, central Australia. Ngarrindjeri is, in fact, the name of the language group; Europeans subsequently used it as a collective name for the lakinyeri following colonization.

Niantic

The Niantic, or in their own language, the Nehântick or Nehantucket were a tribe of New England Native Americans, who lived in Connecticut and Rhode Island. The Niantic were divided into an eastern and western division. The Western Niantic lived just east of the mouth of the Connecticut River while the Eastern Niantic became very close allies to the Narragansett. The division of the Niantic became so great that the language of the eastern Niantic is classified as a dialect of Narragansett while the language of the western Niantic is classified as Pequot-Mohegan.

Nicola (Also see Nlaka'pamux)

The Nicola people are a First Nations political and cultural alliance in the Nicola Valley region of British Columbia. They are mostly located in the Nicola River valley and are an alliance of Scw'exmx, the local branch of the Nlaka'pamux (Thompson) people, and the Spaxomin, the local branch of the Syilx or Okanagan people.

Nimiipuu (Nimi'ipu) (See Nee-me-poo)

Nipmuc

The Nipmuc or Nipmuck people are descendants of the indigenous Algonquian peoples of Nippenet, 'the freshwater pond place', which corresponds to central Massachusetts and immediately adjacent portions of Connecticut and Rhode Island. The various Nipmuc peoples spoke closely related dialects of the Algonquian language family.

Nisenan (Nishinam)

The Nisenan, also known as the Southern Maidu and Valley Maidu, are one of many native groups of the Central Valley of California. The name Nisenan, derives from the ablative plural pronoun nisena·n, "from among us." Nisenan, as with many of the tribes of central California, was never a true political distinction, but in fact is based on a 'common' language (in reality, a wide spectrum on similar dialects).

Nisga'a (Nisgaa, Nishga)

The Nisga'a are a First Nation in Canada that settled their land claim with the British Columbian government on August 4th, 1998. They live in the Nass River valley of northwestern British Columbia.

Declaration of the Nisga'a Nation: We are Nisga'a, the people of K'aliaksim Lisims — From time immemorial we have lived in the lands that K'amligiihahlhat gave to our ancestors. We observe Ayuukhl Nisga'a, we have heard our Adaawak relating to all our Ango'oskw, from the Simgigat and Sigidimhaanak' of each of our wilp. We honour and respect the principle of the common bowl. We are Nisga'a — Since the beginning of time, our leaders have upheld the honour of our nation, and many have grown old and passed on seeking justice for our people. We have heard their stories, we celebrate their loyalty, and we are inspired by their courage. Their struggle was not in vain,their work is now finished, their vision is realized in our time. (Source: http://nisgaanation.ca/)

Nishnawbe Aski

Nishnawbe Aski Nation is a political organization representing 49 First Nation communities across Treaty 9 and Treaty 5 areas of northern Ontario, Canada. Re-organized to its present form in 1981, NAN's original objective was "to represent the social and economic aspirations of our people at all levels of government in Canada and Ontario until such time as real effective action is taken to remedy our problems." Its member-First Nations are Ojibwa, Oji-cree and Cree, thus the languages within NAN include Ojibwe, Oji-cree and Cree. (Source: http://nan.on.ca/article/about-us-3.asp)

Niitsitapi

The Blackfoot Confederacy or Niitsítapi (meaning "original people") is the collective name of three First Nations bands in Alberta, Canada and one Native American tribe in Montana, USA. Originally the Blackfoot Confederacy consisted of three peoples based on kin relationships and dialect, but all speaking a common language, Nitsipussin (Blackfoot) language. These were the Piikáni ("Piegan Blackfeet"), the Káínaa ("Bloods"), and the Siksikáwa ("Blackfoot").

Nlaka`pamux (Nlakapamux)

The Nlaka'pamux or Nlakapamuk, commonly called "the Thompson", and also Thompson River Salish, Thompson Salish, or Thompson River people, are an indigenous First Nations/Native American people of the Interior Salish language group in southern British Columbia. Their traditional territory includes parts of the North Cascades region of Washington.

Nlaka'pamux Nation Tribal Council

We, the Nlaka'pamux Nation Tribal Council are dedicated to protect, assert and exercise our aboriginal rights that will bring about self-sufficiency and well being of our people. This will be accomplished by encouraging and supporting community development which maximizes and enhances our people, culture and resources. Nlaka'pamux Nation Tribal Council Member Bands: Boothroyd Indian Band, Skuppah Indian Band, Lytton First Nation, Boston Bar First Nation, Oregon Jack Creek Band and Spuzzum First Nation. (Source: http://nntc.ca/)

Nomlaki

The Nomlaki (also Noamlakee, Central Wintu, Nomelaki) are a Wintun people native to the area of the Sacramento Valley, Northern California. There are two main groups: The River Nomlaki lived in the Sacramento River region of the valley, and the Hill Nomlaki lived west of the River Nomaki.

Nooksack (Nooksak)

The Nooksack are a Native American people in northwestern Washington State in the United States. The Tribe lives in the mainland northwest corner of the state near the small town of Deming, Washington. The Nooksack language (Lhéchalosem) belonged to the Coast Salishan family of Native American but became extinct around 1988.

Nootka (Nutka) (See Nuu-chah-nulth)

Northern Cheyenne (See Tsististas)

Northern Tutchone

The Northern Tutchone are a First Nations people living mainly in the central Yukon in Canada. The Northern Tutchone language, originally spoken by the Northern Tutchone people, is a variety of the Tutchone language, part of the Athabaskan language family.

Nottoway

The Nottoway (Cheroenhaka), are an Iroquoian-language tribe of Virginia. The Nottoway Indian Tribe of Virginia live from Southampton County into Surry County and the Tidewater region, and the Cheroenhaka (Nottoway) Indian Tribe live in Southampton County and surrounding counties in Virginia and North Carolina. The meaning of the name Cheroenhaka is uncertain. (It has been spelled in various ways: Cherohakah, Cheroohoka or Tcherohaka.)

Nunga

Nunga is a term of self-reference for many of the Aboriginal peoples of southern South Australia.

Nuu-chah-nulth

The Nuu-chah-nulth, also formerly referred to as the Nootka, Nutka, Aht, Nuuchahnulth, are one of the Indigenous peoples of the Pacific Northest Coast of Canada. The term 'Nuu-chah-nulth' is used to describe fifteen separate but related Nations on the west coast of Vancouver Island. The Nuu-chah-nulth are related to the Kwakwaka'wakw, the Haisla, and the Nitinaht. The Nuu-chah-nulth language is part of the Wakashan language group. Nuu-chah-nulth band governments today are: Ahousaht First Nation: (population over 2,000) formed from the merger of the Ahousaht and Kelsemeht bands in 1951; Ehattesaht First Nation; (population 294), Hesquiaht First Nation; (population 653), Kyuquot/Cheklesahht First Nation; (population 486), Mowachaht/Muchalaht First Nations: (population 520) formerly the Nootka band; Nuchatlaht First Nation; (population 165), Huu-ay-aht First Nation: (formerly Ohiaht); (population 598), Hupacasath First Nation (formerly Opetchesaht); (256), Tla-o-qui-aht First Nations: (formerly Clayoquot); (population 881), Toquaht First Nation; (population 117,, Tseshaht First Nation; (population 1002), Uchucklesaht First Nation; (population 181) and Ucluelet First Nation. (population 606).

Nuwu (See Chemehuevi)

Nuxalk

We are the Nuxalk Nation, located in and around what is known to some as Bella Coola, British Columbia, Canada. We have been occupying and exercising our rights on the lands, water and resources of our ancestral territory since time immemorial. The Nuxalk Nation is a mixture of many villages that were distributed throughout kulhulmcilh (our land), including the four largest villages: Talyu in Ats'aaxlh (South Bentick); Suts'lhm (Kimsquit) to the north -this includes Satskw' (Kimsquit River) and Nutl'l (Dean River); Kwalhna to the west; and Q'umk'uts' to the east. (Source: http://nuxalknation.org/content/blogcategory/16/40/)

Nyoongar

The Nyoongar, alternatively spelt Nyungar, Nyoongah, Nyungah, Noonga, or Noongar, are an Indigenous Australian people who live in the south-west corner of Western Australia. The Nyoongar traditionally spoke dialects of the Nyoongar language, a member of the large Pama-Nyungan language family, but generally today speak Australian Aboriginal English, a dialect of the English language interspersed with Nyoongar words and grammar.

Odawa

The Odawa or Ottawa, said to mean "traders," are a Native American and First Nations people. They are one of the Anishinaabeg, related to but distinct from the Ojibwe Nation. Their original homelands are located on Manitoulin Island, near the northern shores of Lake Huron, on the Bruce Peninsula in the present-day province of Ontario, Canada and in the state of Michigan, United States. The Ottawa language is considered a divergent dialect of the Ojibwe.

Ofo (See Mosopelea)

Oglala

The Oglala Lakota or Oglala Sioux, from "to scatter one's own" in Lakota language, are one of the seven sub-tribes of the Lakota people, who along with the Nakota and Dakota, make up the Great Sioux Nation. A majority of the Oglala live on the Pine Ridge Indian Reservation in South Dakota, the eighth-largest Native American reservation in the United States. The Oglala are a federally recognized tribe whose official title is the Oglala Sioux Tribe of the Pine Ridge Reservation.

(Author's Note: Red Cloud is the only Native American Chief to have defeated the Americans in war. Red Cloud's War (1866-68) is also referred to as the Bozeman War or the Powder River War.)

Ogoni

Ogoni people are one of the many indigenous peoples in the region of southeast Nigeria. They share common oil-related environmental problems with the Ijaw people of Niger Delta, but Ogonis are not listed in the list of people historically belonging to Niger Delta. The Ogoni rose to international attention after a massive public protest campaign against Shell Oil, led by the Movement for the Survival of the Ogoni People (MOSOP).

Ohkay Owingeh

Ohkay Owingeh was previously known as San Juan Pueblo until returning to its pre-Spanish name in November 2005. The Tewa name of the pueblo means "place of the strong people." Ohkay Owingeh had a population of 3,357 at the 2000 Census. The entire pueblo has a population of 6,748. The pueblo was founded around 1200 AD during the Pueblo III Era. By tradition, the Tewa people moved here from the north, perhaps from the San Luis Valley of southern Colorado, part of a great migration spanning into the Pueblo IV Era.

Ohlone

The Ohlone people, also known as the Costanoan, are a Native American people of the central and northern California coast. The Ohlone inhabited fixed village locations, moving temporarily to gather seasonal foodstuffs like acorns and berries. The Ohlone people lived in Northern California from the northern tip of the San Francisco Peninsula down to Big Sur in the south, and from the Pacific Ocean in the west to the Diablo Range in the east.

Ojibwe (Ojibway, Ojibwa)

The Ojibwe (also Ojibwa or Ojibway) or Chippewa (also Chippeway) are among the largest groups of Native Americans–First Nations north of Mexico. They are divided between Canada and the United States. In Canada, they are the second-largest population among First Nations, surpassed only by Cree. The Ojibwe peoples are a major component group of the Anishinaabe-speaking peoples, a branch of the Algonquian language family.

Oji-Cree

The Oji-Cree, Anishinini (plural Anishininiwag) or, less correctly, Severn Ojibwa or Northern Ojibwa, are a First Nation in the Canadian provinces of Ontario and Manitoba, residing in a narrow band extending from the Missinaibi River region in

Northeastern Ontario at the east to Lake Winnipeg at the west. The Oji-Cree people are descended from historical intermarriage between the Ojibwa and Cree cultures, but are generally considered a distinct Nation from either of their parent groups. They are considered one of the component groups of Anishinaabe.

Okanagan (See Syilx)

Okwanuchu

The Okwanuchu were one of a number of small Shastan-speaking tribes of Native Americans in Northern California, who were closely related to the adjacent larger Shasta tribe. The Okwanuchu were speakers of the older Hokan-speaking family of languages, with archaeological sites associated with their range dating back in excess of 5000 years.

Omaha

The Omaha are a federally recognized Native American Tribe which lives on the Omaha Reservation in northeastern Nebraska and western Iowa, United States. They migrated to the upper Missouri area and the Plains by the late 17th century from earlier locations in the Ohio River Valley. The Omaha speak a Siouan language of the Dhegihan branch that is very similar to that spoken by the Ponca.

Oneida

The Oneida or Onayotekaono, meaning "the People of the Upright Stone or standing stone", are a Native American/First Nations people; they are one of the five founding Nations of the Haudenosaunee (Iroquois) Confederacy in the area of upstate New York. The Oneida inhabited a territory of about six million acres in central present-day New York, around Oneida Lake and in current Oneida and Madison counties.

Onondaga

The Onondaga (Onöñda'gega' or the People of the Hills) are one of the original five constituent Nations of the Iroquois (Haudenosaunee) Confederacy. Their traditional homeland is in and around Onondaga County, New York. Known as Gana'dagwëni:io'geh to the other Iroquois Tribes, this name allows people to know the difference when talking about Onondaga in Six Nations, Ontario or near Syracuse, New York. Being centrally located, they were considered the "Keepers of the Fire" (Kayečisnakwe'nì·yu' in Tuscarora) in the figurative longhouse.

O'odham (See Tohono O'odham)

Opata

Opata is the collective name for three indigenous peoples native to the northern Mexican border state of Sonora. Opata territory, the "Opateria", encompasses the mountainous northeast and central part of the state extending to near the border with the United States. Most Opatan towns were situated in river valleys and had an economy based on irrigated agriculture.

Osage

There is not much written about the Osage People before the mid-1600's. The Osages were considered a Siouan people, semi-nomadic in nature and recorded mainly throughout the Missouri and Arkansas area. They were a Nation of people with a familial culture of Northern Plains' Tribes. All Nations east of the Mississippi traveled the Trail of Tears. The Osage were no different. They were removed and settled in Kansas. By the time they negotiated the treaty of 1865, to purchase land in Oklahoma, the Osages had reduced in population by 95%. (Source: Official Website of the Osage Nation - http://osageTribe.com/main_culture_overview.aspx)

Osoyoos Indian Band

Scattered throughout the Okanagan Valley on cliffs and in caves are hundreds of drawings of animals and people known as pictographs. These are evidence of a culture that has flourished in the Okanagan Valley for thousands of years. The Osoyoos Indian Band's land base consists of over 32,000 acres of British Columbia's most beautiful land with stunning vistas, rich agricultural lands, and some of the last large tracts of desert lands left in Canada. The Osoyoos Indian Band is a part of the Okanagan Nation, which includes 6 additional Bands in the Okanagan region. Today more than 400 band members live and work on our reserve, which includes some of the last, large tracts of desert left in Canada. (Source: http://nkmip.com)

Otoe

The Otoe or Oto are a Native American people. The Otoe language, Chiwere, is part of the Siouan family and closely related to that of the related Iowa and Missouri tribes.

Otoe-Missouria

The Otoe-Missouria Tribe of Native Americans is a single, federally recognized Tribe, located in Oklahoma. The Tribe is made up of Otoe and Missouria people. Traditionally they spoke the Chiwere language, part of the Souian language family.

Ottawa (See Odawa)

Ouiatenon (See Wea)

Pacheedaht First Nation

The Pacheedaht First Nation is a First Nations band government based on the west coast of Vancouver Island in British Columbia, Canada. Although the Pacheedaht people are Nuu-chah-nulth-aht by culture and language, they are not a member of the Nuu-chah-nulth Tribal Council and define themselves differently. The government has 4 reserve lands for a total of approximately 180 hectares: Pacheena #1, Gordon River #2, Cullite #3, Queesidaquah #4.

Paipai

The Paipai (Pai pai, Pa'ipai, Akwa'ala, Yakakwal) are an Aboriginal people of northern Baja California, Mexico. Today they are concentrated primarily at the multi-ethnic community of Santa Catarina in Baja California's northern highlands.

Paiute

Paiute or Piute refers to three closely related groups of Native Americans — the Northern Paiute of California, Idaho, Nevada and Oregon; the Owens Valley Paiute of California and Nevada; and the Southern Paiute of Arizona, southeastern California and Nevada, and Utah. The Northern and Southern Paiute both speak languages belonging to the Numic branch of the Uto-Aztecan family of Native American languages.

Palus (Palouse)

The Palus are a Sahaptin tribe recognized in the Treaty of 1855 with the Yakamas. A variant spelling is Palouse, which was the source of the name for the fertile prairie of Washington and Idaho.

Pamlico

The Pamlico (or Pomouik) were a Native American people of North Carolina. They spoke an Algonquian language also known as Pamlico or Carolina Algonquian.

Panamint (See Timbisha)

Pangasinan

The Pangasinan are the eighth largest Filipino ethnolinguistic group. They are the residents or indigenous peoples of the Province of Pangasinan, one of the provinces of the Republic of the Philippines. The term Pangasinan can also refer to the indigenous speakers of the Pangasinan language, or people of Pangasinan heritage.

Pascua Yaqui

Native Americans are the true experts about Indian travels and ways of life. The Yaqui people have used oral traditions to pass their rich history from one generation to the next. This is the history of the Yaqui as told by Ernesto Quiroga Sandoval, Historian, Pascua Yaqui Tribe: The Creator made ocean animals and allowed some to emerge onto land. Some evolved into a short human form: the Surem. These are the early ancestors of the Yaquis. The Surem lived in a time out of mind and were a peace-loving, gentle people who had no need for government. Life in the Sonoran desert was a harmonious perfection for the Surem until God spoke through a little tree and prophesied about new horticultural techniques, Christianity, savage invaders, and disunity. The Surem became frightened about parts of this message and transformed into taller, defensive farming people called Yaquis (Hiakim) or Yo'emem (The People). (Source: http://pascuayaqui-nsn.gov)

Passamaquoddy

The Passamaquoddy (Peskotomuhkati or Pestomuhkati in the Passamaquoddy language) are the First Nations people who live in northeastern North America, primarily in Maine and New Brunswick. The name "Passamaquoddy" is an Anglicization of the Passamaquoddy word peskotomuhkati, the prenoun form (prenouns being a linguistic feature of Algonquian languages) of Peskotomuhkat. Peskotomuhkat literally means "pollock-spearer" reflecting the importance of this fish and the fact that their method of fishing was spear-fishing rather than angling.

Patuxet

The Patuxet are an extinct Native American band of the Wampanoag tribal confederation. They lived primarily in and around the area of what has since been settled as Plymouth, Massachusetts.

Patwin

The Patwin (also Patween, Southern Wintu) are a Wintun people native to the area of Northern California. The Patwin comprise the southern branch of the Wintun group, native inhabitants of California since approximately 500 AD. The Patwin spoke a Southern Wintuan language called Patwin.

Paugussett (Paugusset)

They are one of the numerous Algonquian-speaking Nations who emerged in the coastal areas of the Atlantic. Historically, they occupied a region from present-day Norwalk to New Haven, and from Long Island Sound inland for as far as they could navigate by canoe up the Housatonic and Naugatuck rivers.

Pauquachin First Nation

The Pauquachin (BOḰEĆEN)) First Nation is a First Nations government located on Vancouver Island. They are a member of the Sencot'en Alliance fighting for Native rights. In the 1850s they were signatories to the Douglas Treaties.

Pawnee

Pawnee people (also Paneassa, Pari, Pariki) are a Caddoan-speaking Native American Tribe. Historically, the Pawnee lived along outlying tributaries of the Missouri River: the Platte, Loup and Republican rivers in present-day Nebraska and in northern Kansas. They lived in permanent earth lodge villages where they farmed and left on seasonal buffalo hunts, using tipis while traveling.

Pechanga Band of Luiseno Mission Indians

The Pechanga Band of Luiseño Indians has called the Temecula valley home for more than 10,000 years. The Payomkowishum, or Luiseño People were nearly destroyed by events and actions from first contact with Spanish Missionaries. (Source: Website of the Pechanga Band of Luiseño Indians- http://pechanga-nsn.gov/page?pageId=6)

Pee Dee

The Pee Dee Tribe (also spelled Pedee and Peedee) are a Nation of Native Americans of the southeast United States, especially the Piedmont of present-day South Carolina. The Pee Dee River and the Pee Dee region of South Carolina were named for the Nation. Scholars are unsure of what language they spoke, although it may have been of the Siouan family.

Pehuenche

Pehuenches (people of pehuén in Mapudungun) are an indigenous people that are part of the Mapuche peoples and live in the Andes in south central Chile and Argentina. Their name derives from their habit of harvesting of piñones, the seeds of the Araucaria araucana or pehuén. Pehuenches incorporated horse meat into their diet after feral horses of Spanish origin reached the eastern foothills of the Andes.

Pend d'Oreilles

The Pend d'Oreilles, also known as the Kalispel, are a Tribe of Native Americans who lived around Lake Pend Oreille, as well as the Pend Oreille River, and Priest Lake; although, some of them live spread throughout Montana and eastern Washington. The Kalispel are one of the three Tribes of the Confederated Salish and Kootenai Tribes of the Flathead Nation. The name Pend d'Oreille is of French origin meaning "hangs from ears", which refers to the large shell earrings that these people wore.

Penobscot (Pentagoet)

The Penobscot (Panawahpskek) are a sovereign people indigenous to what is now Maritime Canada and the northeastern United States, particularly Maine. They are part of the Wabanaki Confederacy, along with the Abenaki, Passamaquoddy, Maliseet, and Mi'kmaq Nations. The word "Penobscot" originates from a mispronunciation of their name "Penawapskewi" and means "rocky part" or "descending ledges" and originally referred to a portion of the Penobscot River.

Peoria

The Peoria Tribe of Indians of Oklahoma is a confederation of Kaskaskia, Peoria, Piankeshaw and Wea Indians united into a single tribe in 1854. The tribes which constitute The Confederated Peorias, as they then were called, originated in the lands bordering the Great Lakes and drained by the mighty Mississippi. They are Illinois or Illini Indians, descendants of those who created the great mound civilizations in the central United States two thousand to three thousand years ago. Forced from their ancestral lands in Illinois, Michigan, Ohio and Missouri, the Peorias were relocated first in Missouri, then in Kansas and, finally, in northeastern Oklahoma. There, in Miami, Ottawa County, Oklahoma is their tribal headquarters. (Source: http://peoriatribe.com/history.php)

Pequot

Pequot people are a Tribe of Native Americans who, in the 17th century, inhabited much of what is now Connecticut. They were of the Algonquian language family. The Pequot War and Mystic massacre reduced the Pequot's sociopolitical influence in southern New England. Smallpox and other diseases further reduced their numbers and consequestly their influence.

Piankeshaw

The Piankeshaw (or Piankashaw) Indians were Native Americans, and members of the Miami Indians who lived apart from the rest of the Miami nation. They lived in an area that now includes western Indiana and Ohio, and were closely allied with the Wea Indians. Piankashaw villages have been reported along the White River in central Indiana, and along the Vermilion River in Illinois, near Ouiatenon. The Piankashaw were living along the Vermilion river in 1743. (soure: http://yomi.mobi/egate/Pankishaw/a)

Picuris

Picuris Pueblo is a census-designated place (CDP) in Taos County, New Mexico, United States. The population was 86 at the 2000 census. The Pueblo people are from the Tiwa ethnic group of Native Americans. Picurís Pueblo is a member of the Eight Northern Pueblos. Picuris village has occupied its present location since around 750 CE. The Picuris people previously lived in an earlier, larger village now known as Pot Creek, near Taos.

Piegan (Piikani and Peigan)

The Piegan Blackfeet (Aamsskáápipikani (Southern Piikáni/Peigan) or simply as Piikáni in Blackfoot, are a tribe of Native Americans of the Algonquian language family based in Montana, having lived in this area since around 6,500 BC. Many members of the tribe live as part of the Blackfeet Nation in northwestern Montana, with population centered in Browning.

Pima

The Pima (or Akimel O'odham also spelled Akimel O'otham) are a group of Native Americans living in an area consisting of what is now central and southern Arizona. The short name, "Pima" is believed to have come from the phrase pi 'añi mac or pi mac, meaning "I don't know," used repeatedly in their initial meeting with Europeans.

Pipil

The Pipils or Cuzcatlecs are an indigenous people who live in western El Salvador that they called Cuzcatlán. Their language is called Nahuat or Pipil, related to Nahuatl.

Piscataway

The Piscataway are a subTribe of the Conoy Native American Tribe of Maryland. At one time, they were one of the most populous and powerful Native polities of the Chesapeake Bay region. They spoke Algonquian Piscataway, a dialect of Nanticoke.

Pit River

The Pit River Tribe is a federally recognized tribe of eleven bands of indigenous peoples of California. They primarily live along the Pit River in the northeast corner of California. Their name also is spelled as "Pitt River" in historical records.

Pocomoke

The Pocomoke, an Eastern woodland culture, is an Algonquian Tribe who live on what is now known as the Eastern Shore of Maryland. The Pocomoke and the Wicocomico were considered brother Tribes.

Pocumtuck

The Pocumtuck, also Pocomtuc or Deerfield Indians, ere a Native American Tribe formerly inhabiting western Massachusetts. Their territory also included parts o Hampden and Hampshire County, as well as portions of Connecticut and Vermont. Their language, now extinct, was a dialect of the Algonquian language family.

Pojoaque

Pojoaque is a census-designated place in Santa Fe County, New Mexico. Pojoaque and Pojoaque Pueblo are neighbouring communities. Pojoaque Pueblo is an Indian Reservation, and the town of Pojoaque is a collection of communities near the Pueblo with people from various ethnic backgrounds.

Pomo (Pomoan)

The Pomo people are an indigenous people of California. The historic Pomo territory in northern California was large, bordered by the Pacific Coast to the west, extending inland to Clear Lake, and mainly between Cleone and Duncans Point. The people called Pomo were originally linked by location, language, and cultural expression. They were not socially or politically linked as one large unified group.

Ponca

The Ponca are a Native American people of the Dhegihan branch of the Siouan-language group. There are two federally recognized Ponca Tribes: the Ponca Tribe of Nebraska and the Ponca Tribe of Indians of Oklahoma. Their traditions and historical accounts suggest they originated as a Tribe east of the Mississippi River in the Ohio River valley area and migrated west for game and as a result of Iroquois wars.

Popoluca (Popoloca)

Popoluca is a Nahuatl term (meaning "gibberish, unintelligible speech") for various indigenous peoples of southeastern Veracruz and Oaxaca. Many of them speak languages of the Mixe–Zoque family. Others speak the unrelated Mazatecan languages, in which case the name in English and Spanish is generally spelled Popoloca. The reason for the terms widespread usage for naming indigenous languages is that it is a derogatory word from the Nahuatl language meaning "to speak unintelligible" or "gibberish." When Spanish conquistadors asked their Nahuatl-speaking allies what language was spoken in a particular locality, the Nahuas would reply "popoloca" meaning in essence "not Nahuatl." The Nahuas used the term "popolōca" much in the same way the Greek used the term "barbaros", also meaning "gibberish", to refer to non-Greek speaking strangers.

Potawatomi (Pottawatomie)

The Potawatomi, also spelled Pottawatomie and Pottawatomi (among many variations), are a Native American people of the upper Mississippi River region. They traditionally speak the Potawatomi language, a member of the Algonquian family. In the Potawatomi language, they generally call themselves Bodéwadmi, a name that means "keepers of the fire" and that was applied to them by their Anishinaabe cousins. The Potawatomi were part of a long-term alliance, called the Council of Three Fires, with the Ojibwe (Chippewa) and Ottawa. In the Council of Three Fires, the Potawatomi were considered the "youngest brother".

Powhatan

The Powhatan (also spelled Powatan and Powhaten) is the name of a Virginia Indian confederation of Tribes. It may also refer to the leader of those Tribes, commonly referred to as Chief Powhatan. They were also known as Virginia Algonquians, as they spoke an eastern-Algonquian language known as Powhatan or Virginia Algonquin.

Pueblo

The Pueblo people are a Native American people in the Southwestern United States. Their traditional economy is based on agriculture and trade. When first encountered by the Spanish, they were living in villages that the Spanish called pueblos, meaning "towns." The main Pueblos are located primarily in New Mexico and Arizona.

Putún (See Chontal)

Puyallup

In the old days, in our Aboriginal language, we were known as the S'Puyalupubsh, meaning "generous and welcoming behavior to all people (friends and strangers) who enter our lands." We are part of the Salish speaking people of the Pacific Northwest. Our particular dialect is called the "Lushootseed." Our people lived in villages from the foothills of Mount Tacoma, along the rivers and creeks to the shores of Puget Sound. (Source: Official Tribal Homepage - http://puyallup-Tribe.com/history/historical_overview/)

Q'anjob'al

The Q'anjob'al (Kanjobal) are a Maya people in Guatemala. Their indigenous language is also called Q'anjob'al.

Qayqayt First Nation

The Qayqayt First Nation (pronounced Ka-Kite), also known as the New Westminster Indian Band, is a band government located at New Westminster, British Columbia. The Qayqayt First Nation historically spoke the Halq'emeylem (Upriver) dialect of Halkomelem, a Coast Salish language. The Qayqayt reserve used to exist on the banks of the Fraser River, around New Westminster. The Qayqayt First Nation is one of the smallest First Nations in Canada and the only one registered without a land base.

Qualicum

The Qualicum First Nation is a First Nations government located near Qualicum Beach on Vancouver Island, British Columbia, Canada.

Quapaw (Quapa)

The Quapaw people settled in the area where the Arkansas River met the Mississippi, and the meandering of the two massive rivers had deposited nutrient-rich soil conducive to farming. They settled into four villages at the mouth of the Arkansas River. This is where the Quapaw stayed until they were pushed out by European-Americans several hundred years later. (Source: Quapaw Tribe, OK - Official Website - http://quapawTribe.com/index.aspx?nid=85)

Quasmigdo (See Bidai)

Quechan

The Quechan (Quechan: Kwtsaan - "those who descended", spelled "kwuh-tsan", also in English, Kwtsan, Kwtsaan) are a Native American Tribe who live on the Fort Yuma Indian Reservation on the lower Colorado River in Arizona and California just north of the border with Mexico. The Quechan language is part of the Yuman language family.

Quechua

Quechuas (also Runakuna, Kichwas, and Ingas) is the collective term for several indigenous ethnic groups in South America who speak a Quechua language (Southern Quechua mainly), belonging to several ethnic groups in South America, especially in Peru, Ecuador, Bolivia, Chile, Colombia and Argentina. A large bulk of the Chilean population is of Quechua descent; thus many of the words of the Chilean Spanish vocabulary evolved from the language of the Quechua people.

Quilcene

Quilcene is in Jefferson County, Washington. The community is located on the scenic Olympic Peninsula along the seawater-filled glacial valley of the Hood Canal. Early inhabitants of the area were the Twana, inhabiting the length of the Hood Canal. The Quilcene ("salt-water people") were a distinct band of these people.

Quileute

The Quileute, also known as the Quillayute, are a Native American people in western Washington state in the United States. The Quileute language belongs to the Chimakuan family of languages among Northwest Coast indigenous peoples and is one of a kind and is one of only 6 known languages lacking nasal sounds (i.e., m and n). Historically the Quileutes were very talented builders and craftsmen and were excellent boat makers.

Quinault

The Quinault are a group of Native American peoples from western Washington in the United States. There is an original Quinault language, which is a part of the Salishan family of languages. The mixture of members with ethnic ties to the modern Quinault Tribe is made up of the Quinault, Hoh, Chehalis, Chinook, Cowlitz, Queets, and Quileute peoples.

Quinnipiac (See Eansketambawg)

Quiripi (See Eansketambawg)

Raramuri (See Tarahumara)

Restigouche (See Mi'kmaq)

Roanoke

The Roanoke, also spelled Roanoac, tribe were a Carolina Algonquian-speaking people whose territory comprised present-day Dare County, Roanoke Island and part of the mainland at the time of English exploration and colonization. They were one of the numerous Carolina Algonquian tribes, which may have numbered 5,000-10,000 people in total in eastern North Carolina at the time of English encounter. The last known chief of the Roanoke was Wanchese, who traveled to England with colonists in 1584. The smaller Croatan people may have been a branch of the Roanoke or a separate tribe allied with it.

Rumsen

The Rumsen people (also known as Rumsien, San Carlos Costanoan and Carmeleno) are one of eight groups of Ohlone people, also known as Costanoan, indigenous peoples of California.

Saanich (See WSÁNEĆ)

Sac

The Sacs or Sauks are a group of Native Americans of the Eastern Woodlands culture group. Their autonym is (oθaakiiwaki in their own language), and their exonym is Ozaagii(-wag) in Ojibwe. The latter is the source of their names in French and English.

Sahaptin

The Sahaptin peoples were a number of Native American tribes that spoke dialects of the Sahaptin language group. The Sahaptin tribes inhabited territory along the Columbia River in the Pacific Northwest region of the United States. Sahaptin-speaking peoples included the Nez Perce, Umatilla, Tenino, and Yakama.

Sahtu

The Sahtú (or North Slavey, Hare) are an Aboriginal Dene people living in the vicinity of Great Bear Lake (Sahtú, the source of their name), Northwest Territories, Canada. Sahtú groups include the Hare (K'ahsho Got'ine District), Bear Lake (Déline District), and Mountain (Tulit'a District).

Saik'uz First Nation

Saik'uz First Nation is a Dakelh community a short distance from the geographical center of British Columbia. The name Saik'uz is derived from the Dakelh (Carrier) word 'on the sand' and refers to the sandy soil upon which the main community is located. (on Reserve No. 1 on the east end of Nulki Lake on Tachick lake 14 km south of Vanderhoof, BC.) (Source: http://saikuz.com)

Salhulhtxw (See Sliammon)

Salinan

The Salinan Native Americans lived in what is now the Central Coast of California, in the Salinas Valley. There were two major divisions, the San Miguel (Migueleño) in the south and the San Antonio (Antoniaño) in the north. There were also a Playano group which lived on the Pacific Coast. The Salinan language, spoken until the 1950s, is a language isolate.

Salish

The Salish peoples are an ethno-linguistic group of the Pacific Northwest, identified by their use of the Salish languages. Salish is an Anglicization of seliš, the endonym for the Salish Tribes of the Flathead Reservation. The seliš were the easternmost Salish people and the first to have a diplomatic relationship with the United States so their name was applied broadly to all peoples speaking a related language.

Sami

The Sami people, also spelled Sámi or Saami, are the indigenous people inhabiting the Arctic area of Sápmi, which today encompasses parts of far northern Sweden, Norway, Finland, the Kola Peninsula of Russia. Traditionally, the Sami have pursued a variety of livelihoods, including coastal fishing, fur trapping and sheep herding. Their best-known means of livelihood is semi-nomadic reindeer herding.

Sammamish

The Sammamish people were a Coast Salish Native American tribe in the Sammamish River Valley in central King County, Washington. Their name is variously translated as "meander dwellers"" or "willow people." They were also known to early European-American settlers as "Squak", "Simump" and "Squowh." The Sammamish originally spoke a southern dialect of Lushootseed.

Samish

The Samish Indian Nation is the successor to the large and powerful Samish Nation, a signatory to the Treaty of Point Elliott in 1855. The Tribes traditional territory stretches over a wide seven-county region of Northwest Washington. This area, which ranges from the mountain tops of the Cascades westerly along the hills, woodlands, and river deltas, arriving at the far western shores of the San Juan Islands, which provides a backdrop for our history and cultural traditions that remain strong today. (Source: http://samishtribe.nsn.us/samish-community/culture/)

San

The indigenous people of Southern Africa, whose territory spans most areas of South Africa, Zimbabwe, Lesotho, Mozambique, Swaziland, Botswana, Namibia, and Angola, are variously referred to as San, Sho, Basarwa, Kung, or Khwe. These people were traditionally hunter-gatherers, part of the Khoisan group and are related to the traditionally pastoral Khoikhoi.

Sandia Pueblo

The Pueblo of Sandia is a federally recognized Tribe located in central New Mexico and adjacent to Albuquerque, the largest metropolitan area in New Mexico. The reservation covers 22,877 acres on the east side of the Rio Grande Valley. Sandia Pueblo is one of 19 pueblos located throughout New Mexico. The Sandia people are members of the pre-Columbian Tiwa language group who once dominated the Albuquerque area and their lineage can be traced back to the Aztec civilization who later migrated to the New Mexico region. The present site has been home to the Sandia people, where they have cultivated the land and raised their families, since 1300 AD. The Sandia Mountain provides the source of their spirituality as well as plants, animals and other resources which have been critical to their survival in this desert region. Once the largest pueblo in the area with over 3000 people, they currently have just under 500 members. (Source: http://sandiapueblo.nsn.us/home.html)

San Felipe Pueblo

San Felipe Pueblo (Eastern Keres: Katishtya) is in Sandoval County, New Mexico. The Pueblo, founded in 1706, comprises Native Americans who speak an eastern dialect of the Keresan languages. The Pueblo celebrates the annual Feast of St. Philip on May 1, when hundreds of pueblo people participate in traditional corn dances.

San Ildefonso Pueblo

San Ildefonso Pueblo is in Santa Fe County, New Mexico. San Ildefonso Pueblo is a member of the Eight Northern Pueblos, and the pueblo people are from the Tewa ethnic group of Native Americans, who speak the Tewa language. The traditional name for San Ildefonso Pueblo is Po-woh-ge-oweenge, meaning "where the water cuts through."

Sanish (Sahnish) (See Arikara)

San Juan Southern Paiute Tribe

The San Juan Southern Paiute Tribe is the newest federally recognized Native American Nation in the State of Arizona. They live in Coconino County, Arizona. Although they lived by the Hopi and Navajo people, the San Juan Southern Paiutes maintained their own distinct language and culture.

Sanpoil

The Sanpoil (or San Poil) is one of 12 Aboriginal Confederated Tribes of the Colville Indian Reservation. The name Sanpoil comes from the Okanagan, "gray as far as one can see."

Santa Ana Pueblo

Santa Ana Pueblo (Eastern Keres: Tamaiya) is in Sandoval County, New Mexico. The Pueblo, named Tamaya in the native language, is composed of Native Americans who speak an eastern dialect of the Keresan languages. The pueblo celebrates an annual feast day for its patron saint, St. Anne, on July 26.

Santa Clara Pueblo

Santa Clara Pueblo (Tewa: Kha'po) is in Rio Arriba County, New Mexico. The pueblo is a member of the Eight Northern Pueblos, and the people are from the Tewa ethnic group of Native Americans who speak the Tewa language. Santa Clara Pueblo is famous for producing hand-crafted pottery, specifically blackware and redware with deep engravings.

Santee

The Santee Indian Organization, a remnant tribe, was officially recognized by the South Carolina Commission for Minority Affairs on January 27, 2006. Historically, the Santee were a small tribe (est. at a population of 3000 around 1600 AD), speaking a Siouan language and centered in the area of the present town of Santee, South Carolina. Their settlement was along the Santee River, since dammed and called Lake Marion.

Santiam

Santiam people are an indigenous people of the Northwest Plateau, living in Oregon. They are a Kalapuyan tribe, whose traditional homelands were on the banks of the Santiam River, which feeds into the Willamette River. Today, they are enrolled in the Confederated Tribes of the Grand Ronde Community and the Confederated Tribes of Siletz Indians.

Santo Domingo Pueblo (See Kewa)

Saponi

Saponi is one of the eastern Siouan-language Tribes, related to the Tutelo, Occaneechi, Monacan, Manahoac and other eastern Siouan peoples. Its ancestral homeland was in North Carolina and Virginia. The Tribe was long believed extinct, as its members migrated north to merge with other Tribes.

Sarcee (Sarsi) (See Tsuu T`ina)

Sastean (Sasta) (See Shasta)

Satsop

The Satsop Native Americans, who lived along the Satsop river in Washington, were neighbours of the Lower Chehalis, Humptulip, and the Hoquiam peoples, with whom they shared a similar political organization. Some classify the Satsops as a subdivision of the Lower Chehalis people while others place them closer to the Upper Chehalis (Kwaiailk) people. There is no Satsop tribe today.

Sauk (See Sac)

Sauk-Suiattle

The Sauk-Suiattle people lived under the gaze of Whitehorse Mountain for many generations. We lived as hunters, gathers and fishermen in the region of Sauk Prairie near the present-day town of Darrington, Washington. In the early days, we were known as the Sah-ku-mehu. (Source: Official Tribal Homepage - http://sauk-suiattle.com/)

Saulteaux

The Saulteaux, also written Salteaux and many other variants, are a First Nation in Ontario, Manitoba, Saskatchewan, Alberta and British Columbia, Canada. The Saulteaux are a branch of the Ojibway Nations. They are sometimes called the Anihšināpē (Anishinaabe). Saulteaux is a French term meaning "people of the rapids," referring to their former location in the area of Sault Ste. Marie.

Savannah (See Shawnee)

Schaghticoke (Scaticook)

The Schaghticoke are a Native American Tribe of the Eastern Woodlands consisting of descendants of Mahican (also called "Mohican", but not to be confused with the Mohegans), Potatuck (or Pootatuck), Weantinock, Tunxis, Podunk, and other people indigenous to what is now Connecticut, New York, and Massachusetts. They amalgamated after encroachment of white settlers on their ancestral lands.

Scia'new (Cheauth) First Nation (See WṢÁNEĆ)

Scw'exmx

The Scw'exmx, meaning "people of the creek(s)", are a branch of the Nlaka'pamux (Thompson) people in the Nicola Country of the Canadian province of British Columbia. "Scw'ex", meaning "creek", is the name of the Nicola River in the Nlaka'pamux language. Together with the neighbouring branch of the Okanagan people the Spaxomin (usually Spahomin in English), who live in the upper, eastern reaches of the Nicola Valley, they are generally known in English as the Nicolas. They also share governmental institutions, and their alliance dates to before the time of Chief Nicola, for whom the river was named and whose father had led the Okanagan migration into the valley in the late 18th Century. The Scw'exmx intermarried with the Okanagans, and also with the Stu'wix, a now-extinct Athapaskan-speaking people who migrated into the valley in the 17th Century.

Sechelt

The Sechelt (Shíshálh) First Nation, located on BC's scenic West Coast is proud of our heritage and community values. Our spectacular scenery and natural resoures in the territory have sustained our people and way of life for centuries. We thrive on a communal lifestyle that respects the wisdom of our elders. Shíshálh Nation Vision To achieve self-reliance and independence for the Shíshálh Nation we recognized that our collective success depends on knowing our history, understanding our present circumstances and charting a path that leads towards a healthy and prosperous future. In 1986 the Shíshálh Nation became an independent self-governing body... a unique third order of the government of Canada. The Sechelt Indian Government District holds jurisdiction over its lands and exercises the authority to provide services and education for its residents. (Source: http://secheltnation.ca/)

Secwepemc (Secwepmectsin)

The Secwepemc People, known by non-natives as the Shuswap, are a Nation of 17 bands occupying the south-central part of the Province of British Columbia, Canada. The ancestors of the Secwepemc people have lived in the interior of British Columbia for at least 10,000 years. At the time of contact with Europeans in the late 18th century, the Secwepemc occupied a vast territory, extending from the Columbia River valley on the east slope of the Rocky Mountains to the Fraser River on the west and from the upper Fraser River in the north to the Arrow Lakes in the south. Traditional Shuswap territory covers approximately 145,000 square kilometres (56,000 square miles). The

Nation was a political alliance that regulated use of the land and resources, and protected the territories of the Shuswap. Although the bands were separate and independent, they were united by a common language - Secwepemctsin - and a similar culture and belief system. (Source: http://secwepemc.org/about/ourstory)

Sekani

Carrier and Sekani people historically have resided in a vast territory, of over 76,000 kilometers, primarily located in North Central British Columbia. Today there are approximately 22 Indian Bands or First Nations, as recognized by the Department of Indian Affairs that identify as being Carrier or Sekani societies. The population represented by Carrier Sekani First Nations comprises over 10,000 individuals. Among the Carrier and Sekani people there are distinct groupings which maintain geographic and linguistic characteristics different from other groupings of Carrier people. Current research divides Carrier into two major dialect groups within the Athabaska language family, a Stuart-Trembleur Lake group, and a Southern group.

Within the Stuart-Trembleur Lake sub group there are six distinct Carrier linguistic dialects of the Athabaskan language family: Babine, Cheslatta, Nakazd'li, Saik'uz, Lheidli-T'enneh and Wet'suwet'en. Carrier people maintain a governance system commonly referred to as the bah'lats or potlatch. Four primary clans make up Carrier society Likh ji bu (Bear), Gilhanten (Caribou), Jihl tse yu (Frog), and Likh sta Mis yu (Beaver), each with several sub-clans. Members of the Carrier Sekani Tribal Council include: Nadleh Whut'en, Nak'azdli Band, Stellat'en First Nation, Saik'uz First Nation, Takla Lake First Nation, Tl'azt'en Nation, Ts'il Kaz Koh, Wet'suwet'en First Nation (Sources: http://csfs.org/files/carrier-sekani-nations.php and http://carriersekani.ca/)

Selkirk

The Selkirk First Nation is located at the village of Pelly Crossing on the Klondike Highway in the Central Yukon. The Selkirk First Nation is part of the Northern Tutchone language and cultural grouping and is closely connected with their Northern Tutchone neighbours, the First Nation of Nacho Nyak Dun in Mayo, and the Little Salmon Carmacks First Nation in Carmacks. The three First Nations are formally associated through an organization known as the Northern Tutchone Tribal Council. (Source: Council of Yukon First Nations Website - http://cyfn.ca/ournationssfn)

Semiahmoo (SEMYOME) (See W̱SÁNEĆ)

Seminole

The Seminole are a Native American people originally from Florida, who now reside primarily there and in Oklahoma. The Seminole Nation emerged in a process of ethnogenesis out of groups of other Native Americans and a small number of escaped slaves. They were composed most significantly of Creek people from what is now Georgia, the Florida Panhandle and Alabama. The word Seminole is a corruption of cimarrón, a Spanish term for "runaway" or "wild one", historically used for certain Native American groups in Florida.

SEMYOME (Semiahmoo) (See W̱SÁNEĆ)

Seneca

The Seneca are a group of indigenous people native to North America. They were the Nation located farthest to the west within the Six Nations or Iroquois League in New York before the American Revolution. The Seneca Nation's own name (autonym) is Onöndowága, meaning "People of the Great Hill".

Seri

The Seris are an indigenous group of the Mexican state of Sonora. They were historically seminomadic hunter-gatherers. It is one of the ethnic groups of Mexico that has most strongly maintained its language and culture. The Seri people are not related culturally or linguistically to other groups that have lived in the area. The Seri language is distinct from all others in the region and is considered a linguistic isolate. The name Seri is an exonym of uncertain origin. Their name for themselves is Comcaac.

Serrano

The Serrano are an indigenous people of California. They use the autonyms of Taaqtam, meaning "people"; Maarenga'yam, "people from Morongo"; and Yuhaviatam, "people of the pines." The Serrano historically lived the San Bernardino Mountains and extended east into the Mojave Desert and north in the San Gabriel Mountains through the Sierra Pelona Mountains to the Tehachapi Mountains in Southern California.

Severn Ojibwe (See Oji-Cree)

Shanel (See Pomo)

Shasta (Shastan)

The Shasta (or Chasta) are an indigenous people of Northern California and Southern Oregon in the United States. They were originally located in the greater Shasta Valley area of Siskiyou County, California. Generally included with the Shasta tribe proper, are a number of adjacent smaller tribes who spoke a related Shastan language. These include the Konomihu, New River Shasta and the Okwanuchu tribes.

Shawnee (Shawano or Shaawanwa)

The Shawnee are an Algonquian-speaking people native to North America. Historically they inhabited the areas of present-day Ohio, Virginia, West Virginia, Western Maryland, Kentucky, Indiana, and Pennsylvania in the United States.

Note: Tecumseh (Meaning Shooting Star or Panther across the sky -March 1768 – October 5, 1813) is one of the most famous Native leaders of the late 18th and early 19th Centuries. He formed one of the largest and wide ranging confederacies (known as Tecumseh's Confederacy) that opposed the United States during Tecumseh's War and the War of 1812. Tecumseh has become an iconic folk hero in American, Aboriginal and Canadian history.

Shinnecock

Shinnecock are an Algonquian people from Long Island. The Shinnecock are believed to have spoken a dialect of Mohegan-Pequot-Montauk, similar to their neighbours the Montaukett on Long Island. The languages became extinct sometime in the mid-19th century, as numbers of native speakers were drastically reduced.

Shipibo

The Shipibo-Conibo are an indigenous people along the Ucayali River in the Amazon rainforest in Perú. Formerly two groups, the Shipibo (apemen) and the Conibo (fishmen), they eventually became one distinct Tribe through intermarriage and communal ritual. Many of their traditions are still practiced, such as ayahuasca shamanism. Shamanistic songs have inspired artistic tradition and decorative designs found in their clothing, pottery, tools and textiles.

Shoshone (Shoshoni)

The Shoshone or Shoshoni are a Native American Tribe in the United States with three large divisions: the Northern, the Western and the Eastern. They traditionally spoke the Shoshoni language, a part of the Numic languages branch of the large Uto-Aztecan language family. The Shoshone were sometimes called the Snake Indians by early ethnic European trappers, travelers, and settlers. The most historically well-known member of the Shoshone may be Sacagawea, of the Lemhi Shoshone band of Northern Shoshone. She accompanied the Corps of Discovery (Lewis and Clark Expedition) with Meriwether Lewis and William Clark in their exploration of the Western United States. She and Georges Douillard (Métis) are considered to have been instrumental in enabling this expedition to survive. Lewis wrote of Druillard, "he has been peculiarly useful from his knowledge of the common language of gesticulation, and his uncommon skill as a hunter and woodsman." This language of gesticulation was the 'sign language' of trade that was understood from the Floridas to the Pacific Coast. How many thousands of years it took to develop a universal sign language in the time before the horse or the train is a question that did not seem to occur to either Lewis or Clark.

Shuar

The Shuar people are an indigenous people of Ecuador and Peru. They are members of the Jivaroan peoples, who are Amazonian Tribes living at the headwaters of the Marañón River. Shuar, in the Shuar language, means "people."

Shuswap (See Secwepemc)

Siksika (Siksikáwa)

The Siksika Nation is a First Nation in southern Alberta, Canada. The name Siksiká comes from the Blackfoot words sik (black) and iká (foot). The plural form of Siksiká is Siksikáwa. The Siksikáwa are the northernmost of the Niitsítapi (Original People), all of whom speak dialects of Blackfoot, an Algonquian language.

Siletz

The Siletz people are a Native American Tribe from Oregon and an Indigenous people of the Northwest Plateau. Traditionally, they were Salishan-speaking group, who inhabited an area along the central coast of Oregon near the Siletz River. The Tribe was the southernmost group of the larger Coast Salish culture. The Siletz were closely related in language and culture to the Tillamook Tribe.

Similkameen (See Syilx)

Sinkiuse-Columbia

The Sinkiuse-Columbia were a Native American Tribe so-called because of their former prominent association with the Columbia River. They called themselves Tskowa'xtsEnux, or Skowa'xtsEnEx (meaning has something to do with "main valley"), or Sinkiuse. They applied the name also to other neighbouring Interior Salish peoples. The name may have belonged originally to a band that once inhabited the Umatilla Valley.

Sinkyone (See Eel River)

Sioux (See Nadouessioux)

Sisseton Wahpeton Oyate

The Sisseton-Wahpeton Oyate of the Lake Traverse Reservation, formerly Sisseton-Wahpeton Sioux Tribe/Dakota Nation, is a federally recognized tribe comprising two bands and two sub-divisions of the Isanti or Santee Dakota people. They are located on the Lake Traverse Reservation in northeast South Dakota.

Siuslaw

Siuslaw (also Upper Umpqua) is one of the three Confederated Tribes of Coos, Lower Umpqua and Siuslaw Indians located on the southwest Oregon Pacific coast in the United States. The Siuslaw language is extinct.

Skagit

The Skagit are either of two tribes of the Lushootseed Native American people living in the state of Washington, the Upper Skagit and the Lower Skagit. They speak a sub-dialect of the Northern dialect of Lushootseed, which is part of the Salishan family.

Skicin (See Maliseet)

S'Klallam (See Klallam)

Skokomish

What is now known as the Skokomish Tribe actually was primarily composed of Twana Indians, a Salishan people whose Aboriginal territory encompassed the Hood Canal drainage basin in western Washington State. There were nine Twana communities, the largest being known as the Skokomish, or "big river people." The Twana subsisted on hunting, fishing and gathering activities, practicing a nomadic life-style during warmer weather and resettling at permanent sites during the winter. (Source: The Skokomish Tribal Nation - http://skokomish.org/frame.htm)

Skraeling

Skræling is the name the Norse Greenlanders used for the indigenous peoples they encountered in North America and Greenland. In surviving sources it is first applied to the Thule people. In the sagas it is also used for the peoples of the region known as Vinland, probably Newfoundland.

Skwxwú7mesh

The Skwxwú7mesh Úxwumixw (Squamish People, villages and community) have a complex and rich history. Ancient connections are traced within our language through terms for place names and shared ceremony among the Salmon Peoples of the cedar longhouse. We are the descendants of the Coast Salish Aboriginal Peoples who lived in the present day Greater Vancouver area, Gibson's landing and Squamish River watershed. The Squamish Nation has occupied and governed our territory since beyond recorded history.

Sixteen Síiyam (Chiefs) remain from a long line of leaders, and current Skwxwú7mesh generations can trace their connections to one or more of the strong leaders and speakers who signed the Almagamation on July 23, 1923. The Amalgamation was established to guarantee equality to all Squamish people and to ensure good government. (Source: http://squamish.net/about-us/our-history/)

Slavey (Slave, Slavi) (See Dene)

Sliammon (Sliamon)

The Tla'amin Nation resides just north of the province of Powell River in British Columbia. Sliammon First Nation is one of 20 indigenous Coast Salish tribes inhabiting the coastal regions of western Canada. The Tla'amin people are part of a rich heritage with a history stretching back over 2000 years. Traditional Tla'amin territory was along the northern part of the Sunshine Coast, extending along both sides of the Straight of Georgia. The entire territory occupied an area over 400 square kilometers in size, which consisted of numerous permanent and temporary settlements within the region. The Tla'amin people also ventured outside of their territory to trade with their neighbours. Today the Sliammon reservation lies on a portion of land between

Powell River and Lund directly opposite Harwood Island (also reserve land). The community has over 1200 members with the majority living on the reserve. (Source: http://sliammonfirstnation.com/index.php/about-us)

Sm`algyax (See Coast Tsimshian)

Snake

Snake Indians is the common name given by American immigrants on the Oregon Trail to the bands of Northern Paiute, Bannock and Shoshone Native Americans in the Snake River and Owyhee River valleys of southern Idaho and Eastern Oregon.

Snohomish

The Snohomish are a Lushootseed Native American tribe who reside around the Puget Sound area of Washington, north of Seattle. They speak the Lushootseed language. The tribal spelling is Sdoh-doh-hohbsh.

Snoqualmie

The Snoqualmie Tribe — sdukʷalbixʷ in our Native language—consists of a group of Native American peoples from the Puget Sound region of Washington State. Our people have lived in the Puget Sound region since time immemorial. Long before the early explorers came to the Pacific Northwest, our people hunted deer and elk, fished for salmon, and gathered berries and wild plants for food and medicine. (Source: http://snoqualmienation.com/content/about-snoqualmie-Tribe)

Snuneymuxw

The Snuneymuxw First Nation has a rich history and heritage. From the teachings and stories passed down through the generations to the sacred ceremonies, dances, and celebrations that honour our way of life and connection to this land, to the art, designs and symbols that reflect a higher meaning and purpose for our People, our history is a living story that continues to unfold. When Europeans first traveled to Snuneymuxw Territory Snuneymuxw villages dotted all of our Territory, including the mid-Island region of Vancouver Island, Gulf Islands, and the Fraser Valley. Snuneymuxw society, way of life, culture and economy extended throughout the Territory, which was governed by Snuneymuxw according to our Snawaylth. (Source: http://snuneymuxw.ca/nation/history)

Songhees

The Songhees or Songish, also known as the Lekwungen or Lekungen, are an indigenous North American Coast Salish people who reside on southeastern Vancouver Island, British Columbia. The Songhees' traditional foods included salmon, shellfish, whale, deer, duck, berries, camas root, and herbs. The Coast Salish traditionally lived in large cedar buildings that are called longhouse. Today the largest of these types of structures in a community is called the 'Big House.'

Songish (See Songhees)

Sooke (See T`sou-ke)

Souriqouis (See Mi'kmaq)

Southern Paiute

The Southern Paiute traditionally lived in the Colorado River basin and Mojave Desert in northern Arizona and southeastern California, southern Nevada and southern Utah. Terminated as a tribe in 1954 under federal efforts at assimilation, the Southern Paiute regained federal recognition in 1980.

Southern Tutchone

The Southern Tutchone occupies the areas of the southwest Yukon. Many traditional areas and village sites were once the centre of an actively nomadic and trading group of people. While many of these locations were gradually abandoned with the building of the Alaska Highway, they are still regarded with reverence as the homelands of the Southern Tutchone people. (Source: http://cyfn.ca/ourlanguagessoutherntuchone2)

Spaxomin (See Upper Nicola)

Spokane (Spokan)

The Spokane (or Spokan) are a Native American people in the northeastern portion of the U.S. state of Washington. The city of Spokane, Washington takes its name, which means "children of the sun" or "Sun People", from them. Their language belongs to the Interior Salishan family. The Spokane Tribe comprises five bands: sntu/t/uliz, snzmeme/, scqesciOni, sl/otewsi, hu, sDmqeni.

Squamish (See Skwxwú7mesh)

Squaxin

The Squaxin Island Tribe (also Squaxin, Squaxon) is a Native American tribal government in western Washington. The tribe is made up of several Lushootseed clans: the Noo-Seh-Chatl, Steh-Chass, Squi-Aitl, T'Peeksin, Sa-Heh-Wa-Mish, Squawksin, and S'Hotle-Ma-Mish.

St'at'imc (Stl'atl'imx)

The St'át'imc are the original inhabitants of the territory which extends north to Churn Creek and to South French Bar; northwest to the headwaters of Bridge River; north and east toward Hat Creek Valley; east to the Big Slide; south to the island on Harrison Lake and west of the Fraser River to the headwaters of Lillooet River, Ryan River and Black Tusk.The St'át'imc way of life is inseparably connected to the land. Our people use differen locations throughout our territory of rivers, mountains and lakes, planning our trips with the best times to hunt and fish, harest food and gather medicines. The lessons of living on the land are a large part of the inheritance passed on from St'át'imc elders to our children. (Source: http://sttimc.net/)

Stillaguamish

Stillaguamish are a Native American Tribe located in northwest Washington state in the United States near the city of Arlington, Washington, near the river that bears their name, the Stillaguamish River. The Tribe helps manage salmon populations in the Stillaguamish River watershed and has a hatchery which releases chinook and coho salmon. In addition, they voluntarily do not fish for chinook salmon on the Stillaguamish River

Stockbridge-Munsee (See Mohican)

Stó:lō

The Stó:lō Nation Society, as it exists today, evolved from several organizations that emerged in response to the Trudeau government's 1969 Liberal Indian Policy, usually referred to as the White Paper. If successful, the White Paper would have resulted in changes to the Statues of Canada and the British North America Act. The Department of Indian Affairs (DIA) would have ceased to exist and all benefits accorded to Status Indians would have ended. Aboriginal people across Canada would have been assimilated according to federal and provincial government policies. Members of the Nation are: Aitchelitz, Leq'á:mel, Matsqui, Popkum, Skawahlook, Skowkale, Shxwhà:y Village, Squiala, Sumas, Tzeachten and Yakweakwioose. (Source: http://stolonation.bc.ca)

Stoney (See Nakoda)

Sts'ailes

Sts'ailes (formerly Chehalis Indian Band) is located in the upper Fraser Valley of British Columbia. Our name, Sts'ailes, meaning the Beating Heart, comes from halfway up the west side of Harrison Lake. In this spot, Xals, the Transformer, battled a once-powerful shaman called the Doctor and turned him to stone. In an effort to preserve and limit him, Xals broke apart pieces of his body and spread them throughout the territory, creating landmarks. Where his heart landed became known as our village, Sts'ailes. Our culture here in Sts'ailes runs very strong. We take great pride in what we do and how we carry ourselves with our ceremonies and spirituality. We "Live the Culture". We perform many ceremonies such as The First Salmon Ceremony, Ground Breakings for new buildings, we have many drummers with vast knowledge of our traditional songs and talented artists that are very well known in our territory and beyond! (Source: http://stsailes.com)

Stswecem'c Xgat'tem

Stswecem'c Xgat'tem is an economically and politically self-sustaining Secwepemc community living our Secwepemc culture, language and traditions in a healthy and safe environment. The people of Canoe Creek Band were, at one time, two distinct Bands, Canoe Creek and Dog Creek, and when the population declined drastically due to mainly to the smallpox epidemic the two communities were made into one band by DIA in the 1800's. Canoe Creek Band is made up of two communities, Dog Creek and Canoe Creek, but each reserve is administered by the same band office. Both communities are located in a semi remote area southwest of Williams Lake on the east side of the Fraser River. (Source: http://canoecreekband.ca)

Stz'uminus First Nation

Stz'uminus First Nation (formerly known as the Chemainus First Nation) are a Coast Salish People who have lived around the Salish Sea for thousands of years. Our traditional territory on east Vancouver Island includes four reserves of more than 1,200 hectares, much of it bordering the Strait of Georgia and Ladysmith Harbour. Our Nation has 1,300 members with about half living on our reserves. We are a rapidly growing Nation, offering our members a range of opportunities, programs and services. We are a member Nation of the Hul'qumi'num Treaty Group. (Source: http://cfnation.com/)

Sugpiaq (See Alutiiq)

Sukuma

The Sukuma is the largest ethnic group in Tanzania. Sukuma means "north" and refers to "people of the north." The Sukuma refer to themselves as Basukuma (plural) and Nsukuma (singular).

Suma

The Suma (also Zuma and Zumana) lived in northern Chihuahua and the Rio Grande River valley of western Texas. They were nomadic hunter gatherers who practiced little or no agriculture. The Suma are extinct as a distinct people, wiped out by smallpox or absorbed by the Hispanic population and the Apache in the eighteenth and nineteenth centuries.

Suquamish (See Duwamish)

Susquehannock

The Susquehannock (also see Andaste) people were Iroquoian-speaking Native Americans who lived in areas adjacent to the Susquehanna River and its tributaries from the southern part of what is now New York, through Pennsylvania, to the mouth of the Susquehanna in Maryland at the north end of the Chesapeake Bay. Evidence of their habitation has also been found in West Virginia.

Swampy Cree

This group of Cree lives in northern Manitoba along the Hudson Bay coast and adjacent inland areas to the south and west, and in Ontario along the coast of Hudson Bay and James Bay. There are also some members of this group living in eastern Saskatchewan around Cumberland House.

Swinomish

The Swinomish are an historically Lushootseed-speaking Native American Tribe in western Washington state in the United States. The Tribe lives in the southeastern part of Fidalgo Island near the San Juan Islands in Skagit County. The lifestyle of the Swinomish, like many Northwest Coast Tribes, involves the fishing of salmon and collecting of shellfish.

SXIMEŁEŁ (Esquimalt) (See W̱SÁNEĆ)

Syilx

Okanagan (Syilx) people have been here since time immemorial, long before the arrival of the Settlers. The word "Syilx" takes its meaning from several different images. The root word "Yil" refers to the action of taking any kind of many-stranded fiber, like hemp, and rolling it and twisting it together to make one unit, or one rope. It is a process of making many into one. "Yil" is a root word which forms the basis of many of our words for leadership positions, as well. Syilx contains a command for every individual to continuously bind and unify with the rest. This command goes beyond only humans and encompasses all strands of life that make up our land. The word Syilx contains the image of rolling or unifying into one, as well as the individual command which is indicated by the "x" at the end of the word which indicates that it is a command directed at the individual level. The command is for every individual to be part of that stranded unified group, and to continue that twisting and unification on a continuous basis. It is an important concept which underlies our consideration of the meanings of Aboriginal title and rights.

The eight member communities of the Okanagan Nation Alliance are from North to South Upper Nicola Band, Okanagan Indian Band, Westbank First Nation, Penticton Indian Band, Upper Similkameen Indian Band Lower Similkameen Indian Band, Osoyoos Indian Band, and Colville Confederated Tribes. (Source: http://syilx.org)

Tabasco Chontal (See Chontal)

Tachi (Tache)

The Tachi Yokut Indians have inhabited the San Joaquin valley for centuries. Our forefathers made their living peacefully through farming, hunting, fishing, and gathering grains, nuts and fruits. Our lands consisted of fertile valleys, marshlands and rolling foothills. (Source: The Tachi Yokut Tribe - http://tachi-yokut.com/history.html)

Taensa

The Taensa (also Tahensa, Tinsas, Tenisaw, Taënsa, Grands Taensas (in French), Taenso, Takensa, Tenza, Tinza) were a people of northeastern Louisiana. They lived on Lake Saint Joseph west of the Mississippi River, between the Yazoo River and Saint Catherine Creek. Their settlements were in present-day Tensas Parish, Louisiana. The meaning of the name is unknown, although it is believed to be an autonym.

Tagish (See Carcross/Tagish)

Tahltan (See Nahane)

Taidnapam (See Upper Cowlitz)

Taino

The Taínos were seafaring indigenous peoples of the Bahamas, Greater Antilles, and the northern Lesser Antilles. They were one of the Arawak peoples of South America, and the Taíno language was a member of the Arawakan language family of northern South America.

Tainui

Tainui is a tribal waka confederation of New Zealand Māori iwi. The Tainui confederation comprises four principal related Māori iwi of the central North Island of New Zealand: Hauraki, Ngāti Maniapoto, Ngāti Raukawa and Waikato. These Iwi share a common ancestry from Polynesian migrants who arrived in New Zealand.

Takelma

The Takelma (also Dagelma) were a Native American people who lived in the Rogue Valley of interior southwest Oregon, with most of their villages sited along the Rogue River. The name Takelma means "(Those) Along the River."

Takla

Takla Lake Nation is a First Nation based around Takla Lake, British Columbia. It was created by the amalgamation of the Takla Lake and Fort Connelly bands in 1959.

Takudh (See Gwich'in)

Taltushtuntede

A small Tribe from the group Athapaska (narrower group Coquille) that settled along the Galice Creek, in southwest Oregon in the 19th century.

Tamoucougoula

The Avoyel or Avoyelles was a small Natchez-speaking Tribe who inhabited land near the mouth of the Red River in the area of present-day Marksville, Louisiana. The indigenous name for this tribe is Tamoucougoula. The word Avoyel is of French derivation and means either "Flint People" or "the people of the rocks."

Tamyen

The Tamyen people (also spelled as Tamien, Thamien) are one of eight linguistic divisions of the Ohlone (Coastanoan) people groups of Native Americans who lived in Northern California. The Tamyen people spoke the Tamyen language, a Northern Ohlone language, which has been extinct since possibly the early 19th century.

Tanaina (See Dena'ina)

Tanana

The Tanana were an Athabaskan speaking Native American group that lived along the headwaters of the Tanana River in what is now central Alaska. Nomadic hunters, in winter they built skin-covered domed houses. Leadership was clan based and matrilineal. Their economic structure was based on the potlatch.

Tanêks(a) (See Biloxi)

Tano (See Tewa)

Taos Pueblo

Our people have a detailed oral history which is not divulged due to religious privacy. Archaeologists say that ancestors of the Taos Indians lived in this valley long before Columbus discovered America and hundreds of years before Europe emerged from the Dark Ages. Ancient ruins in the Taos Valley indicate our people lived here nearly 1000 years ago. Taos Pueblo is the only living Native American community designated both a World Heritage Site by UNESCO and a National Historic Landmark. (Source: http://taospueblo.com/about)

Tarahumara

The Tarahumara (or Rarámuri) are a Native American people of northwestern Mexico who are renowned for their long-distance running ability. In their language, the term rarámuri refers specifically to the men, women are referred to as mukí (individually) and as omugí or igómale (collectively).

Taroko

The Truku, also romanized as Taroko, people are an Indigenous Taiwanese Tribe. Taroko is also the name of the area of Taiwan where the Truku Tribe resides. Previously, the Truku and the related Seediq people were classified in the Atayal group.

Tataviam

The Tataviam (Tataviam: people facing the sun) are a Native American group in southern California. They traditionally occupied an area in northwest present-day Los Angeles County and southern Ventura County. They were distinct from the Kitanemuk and Gabrielino-Tongva.

T̯Á,UTW̱ (Tsawout) (See W̱SÁNEĆ)

Tawakoni

The Tawakoni are a Native American ethnic group closely related to the Wichitas and who spoke a Wichita dialect of the Caddoan language family. They are currently enrolled within the federally recognized tribe, the Wichita and Affiliated Tribes. Their name translates to "river bend among red sand hills."

Tawas (See Ottawa)

Tawira (Tauira)

The Tawira Miskito are indigenous peoples of Nicaragua. They are a band of Miskito people and live in the southern part of the Mosquito Coast. They are also known as Tauira and Tawira. They speak the Tawira language.

Tehachapi (See Kawaiisu)

Ten`a (See Koyukon)

Tenino

The Tenino people, commonly known today as the Warm Springs bands, are several Sahaptin Native American subtribes which historically occupied territory in Oregon. The Tenino people included four localized subtribes — the Tygh, or "Upper Deschutes;" the Wyam, or "Lower Deschutes;" the Dalles Tenino; and the Dock-Spus, or "John Day."

Tepehuano (Tepecano)

The Tepehuán (Tepehuanes or Tepehuanos, from Nahuatl "People from the Mountains") are an indigenous ethnic group in northwest Mexico. The southern Tepehuán were historically referred to as Tepecanos.

Tesuque

Tesuque is in Santa Fe County, New Mexico. Tesuque Pueblo is a member of the Eight Northern Pueblos, and the Pueblo people are from the Tewa ethnic group of Native Americans who speak the Tewa language.

Tetawken (See Cayuse)

Tetes-de-Boules (See Atikamekw)

Tewa (Tiwa)

The Tewa (or Tano) are a linguistic group of Pueblo American Indians who speak the Tewa language and share the Pueblo culture. Their homelands are on or near the Rio Grande in New Mexico north of Santa Fe. Tewa (also known as Tano) is one of five Tanoan languages spoken by the Pueblo people of New Mexico.

Thompson (See Nlaka'pamux)

Tigua (See Tiwa)

Tillamook (See Clatsop-Nehalem)

Timbisha (Timbasha)

The Timbisha ("Red Rock Face Paint") are a Native American tribe federally recognized as the Death Valley Timbisha Shoshone Band of California. They are known as the Timbisha Shoshone Tribe and are located in south central California, near the Nevada border.

Timucua

The Timucua were a Native American people who lived in Northeast and North Central Florida and southeast Georgia. They were the largest indigenous group in that area and consisted of about 35 chiefdoms, many leading thousands of people. The various groups of Timucua spoke several dialects of the Timucua language.

Tinde (also Tinneh and Dini)

Tinde is what the Apache call themselves and Apache is a collective name given to several culturally related Tribes that speak several variations of the Athapascan language and are of the Southwest cultural area. The Apache separated from the Athapascan in western Canada centuries ago, migrating to the southwestern United States. The Zuni, a Pueblo people, gave them the name Apachu, meaning 'enemy' In their dialects, the Apache call themselves Tinneh, Tinde, Dini, or one of several other variations, all meaning "the people."

Tionontati

The Petún, or Tionontati in their Iroquoian language, were a historical First Nations people closely related to the Wendat (Huron) Confederacy. Their homeland was located along the southwest edge of Georgian Bay, in the area immediately to the west of the Huron territory in Southern Ontario of present-day Canada. French traders called these First Nations people the Petún (tobacco), for their industrious cultivation of that plant.

Tla A'min (See Sliammon)

Tlahuica (See Matlatzinca)

Tla-o-qui-aht (See Nuu-chah-nulth)

Tłįchǫ

In 1921, when Chief Monfwi accepted Treaty 11 on behalf of the Tlicho, he declared that "as long as the sun rises, the river flows, and the land does not move, we will not be restricted from our way of life". These words, and the spirit behind them, have always guided the Tlicho. They capture our Cosmology and guide our future. They led us to achieving the Tlicho Agreement in 2005, that gives the Tlicho its own Government with jurisdiction over Tlicho lands and resources. (Source: http://tlichohistory.com/)

Tlingit

The Tlingit, also spelled Tlinkit, are an indigenous people of the Pacific Northwest. Their name for themselves is Lingít, meaning "People of the Tides." The Tlingit are a matrilineal society that developed a complex hunter-gatherer culture in the temperate rainforest of the southeast Alaska coast and the Alexander Archipelago. An inland subgroup, known as the Inland Tlingit, inhabits the far northwestern part of the province of British Columbia and the southern Yukon Territory in Canada.

Toba

The Toba or Qom are an ethnic group in Argentina, Bolivia and Paraguay. They are part of a larger group of indigenous inhabitants of the Gran Chaco region, called the Guaycurues. The Toba name themselves: Qom-lik, meaning simply "people."

Tohono O'odham

Historically, the O'odham inhabited an enormous area of land in the southwest, extending South to Sonora, Mexico, north to Central Arizona (just north of Phoenix, Arizona), west to the Gulf of California, and east to the San Pedro River. This land base was known as the Papagueria and it had been home to the O'odham for thousands of years. (Source: The Official Web Site of the Tohono O'odham Nation - http://tonation-nsn.gov/history_culture.aspx)

Tolowa

The Tolowa people are a Native American tribe. They still reside in their traditional territories in northwestern California and southern Oregon.

Tongva (See Kizh)

Tonkawa

The Tonkawa are a Native American people indigenous to present-day Oklahoma and Texas. They once spoke the now-extinct Tonkawa language believed to have been a language isolate not related to any other indigenous tongues.

Totonacs

The Totonac people resided in the eastern coastal and mountainous regions of Mexico at the time of the Spanish arrival in 1519. Today they reside in the states of Veracruz, Puebla, and Hidalgo. They are one of the possible builders of the Pre-Columbian city of El Tajín.

Towa (See Jemez)

Tr'ondek Hwech'in

The Tr'ondëk Hwëch'in are a Yukon First Nation based in Dawson City. The citizenship of roughly 1,100 includes descendants of the Hän-speaking people, who have lived along the Yukon River for millennia, and a diverse mix of families descended from Gwich'in, Northern Tutchone and other language groups. Yukon First Nations set the land-claims process in motion during the 1970s. Tr'ondëk Hwëch'in began negotiating their individual land claim in 1991. The Tr'ondëk Hwëch'in Final Agreement was signed on July 16, 1998, and came into effect on September 15, 1998. (Source: http://trondek.ca/aboutus.php)

Tsalagi (Tsa-la-gi) (See Cherokee)

Tsalagiyi Nvdagi

The Tsalagiyi Nvdagi, under the name of Texas Cherokee, signed a treaty with the Republic of Texas on February 23, 1836. Texas violated that treaty when they drove the Texas Cherokee and their related bands from Texas by gun and knife on July 16, 1839, and Chief Diwali (principal chief at that time and known to the whites as Bowles) was killed. Those who survived the massacre, either fled to other locations or hid in the deep forest of East Texas so they would not suffer a similar fate. We are not federally recognized and are not part of the Oklahoma or Eastern Tribes, but we are related by blood. We believe, united as a tribe, we are capable of recovering our culture and traditions for the good of our people, today, and future generations to come. We who have come together to reinstate our tribe are very proud people. We will last as long as there is a drop of Ani-Tsalagi blood left among us. (Source: http://texascherokees.org/)

Tsartlip (WJOŁEŁP) (See WSÁNEĆ)

Tsattine (See Danezaa)

Tsawout (ȾÁ,UTW̱) (See WSÁNEĆ)

Tsawwassen

The Tsawwassen First Nation is a First Nations government whose lands are located in the Greater Vancouver area of the Lower Mainland of British Columbia, Canada, adjacent to the South Arm of the Fraser River and the Tsawwassen Ferry Terminal and just north of the international boundary with the United States at Point Roberts, Washington. The Tsawwassen First Nation is a member government of the Naut'sa mawt Tribal Council. Tsawwassen means land facing the sea.

Tseshaht (See Nuu-chah-nulth)

Tsetsaut

Tsetsaut was an Athabascan language once spoken in the southern coast of Alaska and northwest British Columbia. The Tsetsaut people suffered from displacement, warfare and disease in the late 1800's, and though Tsetsaut descendents still live among the Nisga'a, Tahltan and Kaska tribes, there is no distinct Tsetsaut tribe today, and the language has not been spoken since the 1920's.

Tsetsehestahese (See Cheyenne)

Tseycum (WSÍKEM) (See WSÁNEĆ)

Tsilhqot'in

The Tsilhqot'in National Government was established in 1989 to meet the needs and represent the Tsilhqot'in communities of Tlet'inqox, ?Esdilagh, Yunesit'in, Tsi Del Del and Xeni Gwet'in striving to re-establish a strong political government structure. The communities work as a Nation to continue the fight of our six war Chiefs of 1864. The war Chiefs stood against the Canadian Government in an effort to gain Tsilhqot'in Aboriginal Rights and Title to the lands we call Tsilhqot'in. TNG has a dedicated obligation to its people to establish programs that reflect Tsilhqot'in Culture and Customs in every aspect of governance. (Source: htp://tsilhqotin.ca/aboutng.htm)

Tsimshian (Tsimpshian)

The Tsimshian are an indigenous people of the Pacific Northest Coast. Tsimshian translates to "Inside the Skeena River." Their communities are in British Columbia and Alaska. Their culture is matrilineal with a societal structure based on a clan system, properly referred to as a moiety. The Tsimshian Nation (meaning the Coast Tsimshian) in British Columbia consists of fourteen tribes: the Gitdidzu or Kitasoo (who live at Klemtu, B.C.), the Gitga'at (Hartley Bay, B.C.), the Gitxaala or Kitkatla (Kitkatla, B.C.), the Gitsumkalum (Kitsumkalum, B.C.), the Gits'ilaasü or Kitselas (Kitselas, B.C.). Also there are the allied tribes of Lax Kw'alaams (Port Simpson) including Metlakatla, Giluts'aaw, Ginadoiks, Ginaxangiik, Gispaxlo'ots, Gitando, Gitlaan, Gits'iis, Gitwilgyoots and Gitzaxłaał.

Ts'ishaa7ath (Tseshaht) (See Nuu-chah-nulth)

Tsitsistas (See Cheyenne)

Tsleil-Waututh

We are the Tsleil-Waututh Nation, "The People of the Inlet." We have inhabited the lands and waters of our traditional territory surrounding the Burrard Inlet in British Columbia since time immemorial. Many generations of men, women and children have lived, had families, and thrived in this area, and we have a sacred trust, a commitment to care for our lands and waters. Our vision is to once again put the Tsleil-Waututh face on our traditional territory, to be active participants in all social, economic, cultural, and political activities that take place on our lands by building strong relationships based on trust and mutual respect. (Source: http://twnation.ca/)

Tsnungwe

The Tsnungwe (South Fork Indians, South Hupa, South Fork Hupa) are a Native American people settled along the Trinity River and New River, in Trinity and Humboldt County in California. The Tsnungwe language is a dialect of the Hupa language of their neighbours the Hupa.

T'sou-ke

In the SENĆOŦEN language, the word T'Sou-ke is the name of the Stickleback fish that live in the estuary of the river. Exposure to Europeans through the Hudson's Bay Company saw the name changed first to Soke and then Sooke. That English name is now common and is used for many things including the name of our neighbouring town, the river and basin, the main road. The two T'Sou-ke reserves are on 67 hectares (165 acres) around the Sooke Basin on the Strait of Juan de Fuca. The reserves were allotted by the Joint Reserve Commission in 1877. (Source: http://tsoukenation.com/)

Tsoyaha (See Yuchi)

Tsuu T`ina (Tsuutina)

The Tsuu T'ina Nation (also Tsu T'ina, Tsuut'ina, Tsúùtínà - "a great number of people"; formerly Sarcee, Sarsi) is a First Nation in Canada. Their territory is located on the Indian reserve Tsuu T'ina Nation 145, adjacent to Calgary, Alberta. A strong independent people, their beliefs are embodied in the circle symbolizing the eternal continuity of life, the circle forms the basis of their emblem. The stretched beaver pelt is a symbol of the Beaver people and the two warbonnets represent the separation story of the Athapaskan and the Tsuu T'ina people. The peace pipe means "peace with all people". The broken arrow means "no more wars". (Source: http://tsuutina.ca/Culture/Traditional-Symbols)

Tualatin (See Atfalati)

Tuareg

The Tuareg (also spelled Twareg or Touareg; endonym Imuhagh) are a Berber people with a traditionally nomadic pastoralist lifestyle. They are the principal inhabitants of the Saharan interior of North Africa. Most Tuareg live in the Saharan parts of Niger, Mali, and Algeria. Being nomadic, they move constantly across national borders.

Tubatulabal

The valley of the Kern River, California has been the home of three distinct bands that are collectively named Tübatulabal. The name Tübatulabal (which is loosely translated as "Pine-nut Eaters or Gatherers") has been appended to the tribe by their neighbours to the west (Yokuts). The three bands are the Palegawan , Pakanapul, and Bankalachi "Toloim."

Tulalip

The Tulalip Tribes is a federally-recognized Indian tribe located on the Tulalip Reservation in the mid-Puget Sound area bordered on the east by Interstate 5 and the city of Marysville, Washington; on the south by the Snohomish River; on the north by the Fire Trail Road (140th); and on the west by the waters of Puget Sound. The Tulalip Reservation exterior boundaries enclose a land-base of 22,000 acres, more than 50 percent of which is in federal trust status. The Reservation is rich with natural resources: marine waters, tidelands, fresh water creeks and lakes, wetlands, forests and developable land. The Tulalip Reservation was reserved for the use and benefit of Indian tribes and bands signatory to the Treaty of Point Elliott of January 22, 1855. Its boundaries were established by the 1855 Treaty and by Executive Order of President U.S. Grant dated December 23, 1873. It was created to provide a permanent home for the Snohomish, Snoqualmie, Skagit, Suiattle, Samish and Stillaguamish Tribes and allied bands living in the region. (Source: http://tulaliptribes-nsn.gov/Home/WhoWeAre/AboutUs.aspx)

Tumpisa (Tumbisha, Tumbisha) (See Timbisha)

Tunica

The Tunica people were a group of linguistically and culturally related Native American tribes in the Mississippi River Valley, which include the Tunica (also spelled Tonica, Tonnica, and Thonnica); the Yazoo; the Koroa (Akoroa); and possibly the Tioux.

Tupi

The Tupi people were one of the main ethnic groups of Brazilian indigenous people. Scholars believe they first settled in the Amazon rainforest, but 2,900 years ago they started to spread southward and gradually occupied the Atlantic coast.

Tuscarora

The Tuscarora ("hemp gatherers") are a Native American people of the Iroquoian language family, with members in New York, Canada, and North Carolina. They became the sixth Nation to join the Haudenosaunee (Iroquois) Confederacy.

Tutchone (See Norther Tutchone and Southern Tutchone)

Tutelo

The Tutelo (also Totero, Totteroy, Tutera; Yesan in Tutelo) were Native people living above the Fall Line in present-day Virginia and West Virginia, speaking a Siouan dialect of the Tutelo language. They joined with other Virginia Siouan tribes in the late 17th century and became collectively known as the Tutelo-Saponi.

Tututni (See Coquille)

Twana (See Skokomish)

Twatwa (Twightwee) (See Miami)

Uchee (See Yuchi)

Uchucklesaht (See Nuu-chah-nulth)

Ucluelet (See Nuu-chah-nulth)

Ukomnom (See Yuki)

Umatilla

The Umatilla are a Sahaptin-speaking Native American group who traditionally inhabited the Columbia Plateau region of the northwestern United States, along the Umatilla and Columbia Rivers. Linguistically, the Umatilla people spoke a tongue that was part of the Sahaptin division of the Penutian language family.

Umpqua

Umpqua refers to any of several distinct groups of Native Americans that live in present-day south central Oregon in the United States. The Lower Umpqua Tribe is represented in modern times as one of the three Confederated Tribes of Coos, Lower Umpqua and Siuslaw Indians.

Unama'ki Mi'kmaq (Also see Mi'kmaq)

In eastern Canada, five Unama'ki (Cape Breton Island) Mi'kmaq communities sit along the shores of the Bras d'Or Lakes, a semi-saline water body that opens onto the North Atlantic. The Unama'ki Mi'kmaq were the first Aboriginal people in North America to have prolonged contact with Europeans. This has conferred some advantages, especially in terms of political savvy in confronting a European mindset, but also means that five hundred years of colonization have left the Mi'kmaq facing a number of ecological and socio-economic challenges. In recent years the Unama'ki Mi'kmaq have increasingly become players and stakeholders in the non-aboriginal society of Cape Breton. Most significantly, they have taken a prominent role in the search for solutions for the infamous Tar Ponds of Sydney, Nova Scotia-Canada's most toxic site, left over from generations of steel-making (Gordon 1997). Overall, the Unama'ki Mi'kmaq have made great strides in their development and have received recognition and respect from the surrounding district. They have made a visible, positive impact in the areas of environmental sustainability, tourism and other business development. (Source: http://aboriginalsustainabilitynetwork.org/peoples-places/mikmaq)

Author's Note: Unama'ki (Cape Breton Island) is where the author's great-grandmother increased and practiced her herb lore in her association with the Mi'kmaq people on whose traditional lands she had landed after leaving Ireland during the potato famine in the late nineteenth century.

Unangan (Unangax) (See Aleut)

Unkechaug (Unquachog)

The Unkechaug ("People from beyond the hill") Nation maintains a sovereign relationship with the State of New York, other Indian Nations in the United States and Canada and other foreign powers. The Unkechaug Nation is located on the Poospatuck ("where the waters meet") Reservation in Long Island, NY. (Source: Unkechaug Indian Nation - Our History - http://poospatucksmokeshop.com/history.html)

Upper Chehlais (See Chehalis Tribe)

Upper Cowlitz (See Cowlitz)

Upper Nicola

Upper Nicola Band is located 45 km east of Merritt and 90 km south of Kamloops, British Columbia, Canada. We affirm our place in our nation. This page at UNB.COM will make clear not only our commitment and dedication to our great nation, but to also demonstrate our determination to regenerate ancient ties to our brothers and sisters throughout our nation and to those new ties to families from outside our traditional nation. We intend to do this with respect and humility towards our nation members and we put to all our people, the statement that we are here to work along side each one of you and to regenerate our identities through language, culture, tradition, and modern adaptations of this ever changing world we are living in today and in the coming generations. May our ancestors and our relatives of all creation watch over us, guide us, and invigorate our spirits with wisdom and strength to come together as ONE NATION - a regeneration of the Syilx ways. (Source: http://uppernicolaband.com/)

Ute

Ute people are an indigenous people of the Great Basin, now living primarily in Utah and Colorado. There are three Ute tribal reservations: Uintah-Ouray in northeastern Utah; Southern Ute in Colorado; and Ute Mountain which primarily lies in Colorado, but extends to Utah and New Mexico. The name of the state of Utah was derived from the name Ute. The word Ute means "Land of the sun" in their language. "Ute" possibly derived from the Western Apache word "yudah", meaning "high up."

U'wa

The U'wa people are an indigenous people living in the cloud forests of northeastern Colombia. The U'wa are known to neighbouring indigenous peoples as "the thinking people" or "the people who speak well." They were formerly called Tunebo, but today prefer to be known as U'wa, meaning "people."

Virginian Algonkin (See Powhatan)

Vuntut Gwithcin

The Vuntut Gwitchin is the name of our people which in our language means "people of the lakes." We live in the northernmost community of Old Crow located 128 km (80 miles) north of the Arctic Circle at the confluence of the Crow and Porcupine Rivers in Canada's Yukon Territory. (Source: Vuntut Gwitchin First Nation Government Website - http://vgfn.ca/caribou.php)

Wabanaki

The Wabanaki Confederacy (Wabenaki, Wobanaki - translated roughly as 'People of the First Light' or 'Dawnland') are a native American confederation of five principal Nations: the Mi'kmaq, Maliseet, Passamaquoddy, Abenaki and Penobscot. Members of the Wabanaki Confederacy — the Wabanaki peoples — are located in, and named for, the area they call Wabanaki ('Dawnland'), generally known to European settlers as Acadia. It is now most of Maine, Nova Scotia and New Brunswick, plus some of Quebec south of the St. Lawrence River. The Western Abenaki are located in New Hampshire, Vermont, and Massachusetts.

Wahpekute (See Sioux)

Wailaki (See Athabascan)

Wailatpu (Waylatpu) (See Cayuse)

Walapai (See Hualapai)

Walla Walla

Walla Walla are a Sahaptin indigenous people of the Northwest Plateau of the U.S. The reduplication of the word expresses the diminutive form. The name "Walla Walla" is translated several ways but most often as "many waters."

Wampano (See Eansketambawg)

Wampanoag

Wampanoag people also called Pawkunnakuts, or Wôpanâak, are a Native American Tribe. In the beginning of the 17th century the Wampanoag lived in southeastern Massachusetts and Rhode Island. Wampanoag means "Easterners" or literally "People of the Dawn."

Wanapum

The Wanapum tribe of Native Americans formerly lived along the Columbia River in Washington. The name "Wanapum" is from the Sahaptin wánapam, meaning "river people", from wána, "river", and -pam, "people."

Wappinger

The Wappinger were a confederacy of Native Americans primarily based in what is now Dutchess County, New York, their territory extended east into parts of Connecticut. They were most closely related to the Lenape, both being members of the Eastern Algonquian-speaking subgroup of the Algonquian peoples.

Wappo

The Wappo are an indigenous people of northern California. The Wappo lived by hunting and gathering, and lived in small groups without centralized political authority, in homes built from branches, leaves and mud. Their woven baskets were so well crafted that they were able to hold water.

Warm Springs (See Tenino)

Wasco-Wishram

Wasco-Wishram are two closely related Chinook Indian tribes from the Columbia River in Oregon. Today the tribes are part of the Warm Springs Reservation in Oregon and Confederated Tribes and Bands of the Yakama Nation in Washington. The Wishram and Wasco are Plateau tribes that are closely related and share many cultural aspects of the Northwest Coast tribes. They lived along the banks of the Columbia River, near The Dalles. The Dalles were a prime trading location, and the tribes benefited from a vast trade network. Unfortunately, the 19th century brought non-Indians and European diseases, which took a great toll on the Wasco and Wishram populations. Both tribes were forced by the United States in 1855 to sign treaties ceding the majority of their lands. These treaties established the Warm Springs Reservation.

Washo (Washoe)

The Washoe are a Great Basin Tribe of Native Americans, living in California and Nevada. The name "Washoe" is derived from the autonym waashiw meaning "people from here" in the Washo language. The Washoe language is tentatively regarded as part of the Hokan language family; however, it is also considered to be a language isolate. They are the only Great Basin Tribe whose language is not Numic, so they are believed to have inhabited the region before neighbouring Tribes.

Wauzhushk Onigum (See Chippewa)

Wazhazhe (See Osage)

W̱ĆIÁNEW̱ (Becher Bay) (See W̱SÁNEĆ)

Wea (Also See Miami)

The Wea were a Miami-Illinois-speaking Tribe originally located in western Indiana, closely related to the Miami. The name Wea is used today as a shortened version of their numerous recorded names. The Wea name for themselves (autonym) in their own language is 'Waayaahtanwa', derived from waayaahtanonki, 'place of the whirlpool', their name where they were first recorded being seen and is where they were living at that time.

Wenatchi (Wenatchee)

The Wenatchi Tribe are a group of Native Americans who originally lived in the region near the confluence of the Columbia and Wenatchee Rivers in Eastern Washington State. The Wenatchis (or "P'squosa") were not given reservation land by the federal government.

Wendat (See Wyandot)

Wenro

The Wenrohronon or Wenro were a little-known Iroquoian language-speaking indigenous people in western New York and northwestern Pennsylvania. They appear to have inhabited the upper Allegheny River valley, between the territories of the Seneca and the Neutrals. They were ultimately destroyed by the Iroquois Nations during the Beaver Wars, and were assimilated into the victorious Nations.

Weott (See Wiyot)

Westbank

The Westbank First Nation is a First Nations government in the Okanagan region of the Canadian province of British Columbia, located with the District of West Kelowna. They are a member of the Okanagan Nation Alliance.

Wet'suwet'en

Wet'suwet'en (also known as Hwotsotenne, Witsuwit'en, Wetsuwet'en, Wets'uwet'en) are a First Nations people who live on the Bulkley River and around Broman Lake and Francois Lake in the northwestern Central Interior of British Columbia. Wet'suwet'en, means "People of the Wa Dzun Kwuh River". Governance in Wet'suwet'en culture: Becoming a Hereditary Chief: Before non-native contact, a Wet'suwet'en heir began their journey to becoming a hereditary chief while still inside the mother's womb. Elders, Shaman's and Chiefs would often feel the womb of an expectant mother and determine if the baby was destined to be a future Chief or Shaman. From the time of birth the child would be groomed or tutored to be a wise, strong and responsible leader. (Source: http://wetsuweten.com)

Whilkut

The Whilkut also known as "Redwood Creek Indians" or "Mad River Indians" were an Athapaskan tribe, speaking a dialect similar to the Hupa and Chilula, who inhabited the area on or near the upper Redwood Creek and along the Mad River except near its mouth, up to Iaqua Butte, and some settlement in Grouse Creek in the Trinity River drainage in Northwestern California.

White Clay People (See Gros Ventre)

Wichita (Witchita)

The Wichita people are a confederation of Plains Indians; the Waco, Taovaya, Tawakoni, and Wichita proper. Historically they spoke the Wichita language, a Caddoan language. They are indigenous to Kansas, Oklahoma, and Texas.

Wikchamni (See Yokuts)

Wikwemikong

The Anishnabek people of Wikwemikong are citizens of the Three Fires Confederacy: an alliance of Odawa, Ojibway and Pottawatomi nations. The Odawa inhabited Manitoulin Island or "Mnidoo Mnis" for many years prior to any other tribal settlements; it has been referred to as Odawa Mnis". Manitoulin Island has also been called "Ogemah Mnis", the home of the ancestors as recorded by many chiefs having been buried here. The Ojibway arrived in Wikwemikong during the 1850s era treaties. These families continue to reside and contribute to the community. (Source: http://wikwemikong.ca/index.php?option=com_content&view=article&id=48&Itemid=53)

Willapa (Willopah)

The Willapa were an Athapaskan-speaking people in Washington. Their territory was the valley of the Willapa River and the prairie between the headwaters of the Chehalis and Cowlitz Rivers.

Winnebago (See Ho-Chunk)

Wintu (Wintun)

The Wintu (also Northern Wintun) are Native Americans who live in what is now Northern California. They are part of a loose association of peoples known collectively as the Wintun (or Wintuan). The Wintu language is part of the Penutian language family. Historically, the Wintu lived primarily on the western side of the northern part of the Sacramento Valley.

Wiradjuri

The Wiradjuri or Wirraayjuurray people are a group of indigenous people of Australian Aborigines that were united by a common language and strong ties of kinship. They lived as skilled hunter–fisher–gatherers in family groups or clans scattered throughout central New South Wales.

Wiyot (Wi'yot, Wishosk)

Wiyot people have lived in the Humboldt Bay region of northern California for thousands of years. Wiyot people lived in permanent villages along the waterways which also served as travel and trade routes. Seasonal camps were made on the tribal lands and prairies. (Source: Official Site of the Wiyot Tribe - http://wiyot.com/)

WJOŁEŁP (Tsartlip) (See WṢÁNEĆ)

Wolastoqewi (Wolastoqiyik) (See Maliseet)

WṢÁNEĆ

Saanich is an anglicization of the name of the Saanich people or WṢÁNEĆ. The WṢÁNEĆ are indigenous nations from the north coast of the Olympic Peninsula in Washington, the Gulf and San Juan Islands, southern Vancouver Island and the southern edge of the Lower Mainland in British Columbia. Members of the WṢÁNEĆ (Saanich) Nation are: BOĶEĆEN (Pauquachin), MÁLEXEŁ (Malahat), SEMYOME (Semiahmoo), SXIMEŁEŁ (Esquimalt), T'sou-ke (Sooke), TÁ,UTW̱ (Tsawout), W̱ĆIÁNEW̱ (Becher Bay or Beecher Bay: The Sc'ianew (Cheauth) First Nation), WJOŁEŁP (Tsartlip) and WṢÍKEM (Tseycum)

WṢÍKEM (Tseycum) (See WṢÁNEĆ)

Wuikinuxv

We are the people of the Wuikinuxv Nation. Traditionally we were one of the largest nations on the West Coast. Historical disease, conflict and transfer of members to areas with services unavailable due to location have lead to the decrease in band membership. The membership list is numbered in the hundreds. There are an uncounted number of people who still consider themselves to be Wuikinuxv, but who either do not have "status " as defined by the Indian act, or who are members of other bands. (Source: http://wuikinuxv.net/)

Wyandot (Wyandotte)

The Wyandot people or Wendat, also called Huron, are indigenous peoples of North America. They traditionally spoke Wendat. Early theories placed Huron origin in the St. Lawrence Valley, with some arguing for a presence near Montreal and other St. Lawrence Iroquoian peoples. Recent research in linguistics and archaeology confirm such a historical connection between the Huron and the St. Lawrence Iroquois. Like other Iroquoian peoples, the Huron were farmers who supplemented their diet with hunting and fishing.

Xai'xais (See Kitasoo/Xai'xais)

Xat'súll

The Xat'súll First Nation is a member of the Great Secwepemc Nation, once known as the people of Xat'súll (on the cliff where the bubbling water comes out). Xat'súll (Hat'sull) is the northern most Shuswap tribe of the Secwepemc Nation, which is the largest Nation within the interior of BC. The Xat'súll have stewarded territory ranging from the Coast Mountains to the west, east to the Rocky Mountains. Use of the land brought about contact with neighbouring peoples. As with many other First Nations, the Xat'súll Nation followed a hunting and gathering lifestyle centered in family groups and focused on the Fraser River and the salmon. Patterns of land use were at harmony with the natural processes. (Source: http://xatsullheritagevillage.com)

Xavante

The Xavante (also Shavante, Chavante, Akuen, A'uwe, Akwe, Awen, or Akwen) are an indigenous people within the territory of eastern Mato Grosso state in Brazil. They speak the Xavante language, part of the Jé language family. They were enslaved in the 17th century and they are still wary of any non-Xavante, called "waradzu."

Xaxli'p First Nation

Xaxli'p Formerly known as Fountain Band, is a First Nations government located about 10 miles (15km) from the Village of Lillooet on Highway 99 North, in the Central Interior-Fraser Canyon region of the Canadian province of British Columbia. Xaxli'p is a member of the Lillooet Tribal Council. Other St'at'imc governments include the smaller In-SHUCK-ch Nation on the lower Lillooet River to the southwest, and the independent N'quatqua First Nation at the farther end of Anderson Lake from Seton Portage, which is the location of three of the reserve communities of the Seton Lake FIrst Nation, aka the Seton Lake Indian Band. (Source: http://xaxlip.ca/)

Xa'xtsa

Xa'xtsa is made up of two communities: Port Douglas, which is situated at the northern end of Little Harrison Lake, and Tipella which is on the west side of the Lillooet River. Xa'xtsa is also part of the entire St'at'l'imx linguistic group. The name 'Port Douglas' originates from the colonial period, when the town, one of the earliest to be established in mainland British Columbia, was erected adjacent to the present Xa'xtsa community in 1858. (Source: http://xaxtsa.ca/)

Xeni Gwet'in

The Xeni Gwet'in First Nation is one of six Tsilhqot'in communities which include: Yunesit'in, Tl'etinqox, Tsi Del Del, ?Esdilagh, and Tl'esqox. Welcome to our home. This spectacular region contains some of the purest waters in the world. Since ancient times the Tsilhqot'in People of Xeni have lived here in strength and harmony. Past, present and future generations of people walk this land, fish its waters and harvest through the seasons. The other Tsilhqot'in communities include: Tsi Del Del (Alexis Creek Indian Band), Tl'etinqox't'in (Anaham Indian Band), Tl'esqox't'in (Toosey Indian Band), Yunesit'in (Stone Indian Band), and ?Esdilagh (Alexandria Indian Band). The Tsilhqot'in communities are neighboured by the Nuxalk along the Pacific Coast, the Southern Carrier to the north, Northern Secwepemc to the east and the Lillooet to the south. The Caretaker Area of the Xeni Gwet'in First Nation (honey gwe-teen) is in the Chilko River Watershed, in the Tsilhqot'in Territory (tsil-kote-een), west of the Fraser River. Nemiah Valley is approximately 250 kilometers west of Williams Lake. (Source: http://xeni.ca/Home/AbouttheXeniGwetin/tabid/64/Default.aspx)

Yakama (Yakima)

Upon central Washington's plateau and along the Columbia River reside tribal people called the Yakama's. Yakama people spent the coldest months in winter villages generally located on the valley floor. In the springtime, as soon as the first edible greens appeared above the ground, tribal people began moving across the countryside for fresh food resources. (Source: Official Sire of the Confederated Tribes of the Yakama Nation - http://yakamanation-nsn.gov/history.php)

Yakuts

Yakuts (are a Turkic people who mainly inhabit the Sakha (Yakutia) Republic. The Yakut or Sakha language belongs to the Northern branch of the Turkic family of languages. The Yakuts are divided into two basic groups based on geography and economics. Yakuts in the north are historically semi-nomadic hunters, fishermen, reindeer breeders, while southern Yakuts engage in animal husbandry focusing on horses and cattle.

Yamasee

The Yamasee were a multiethnic confederation of Native Americans who lived in the coastal region of present-day northern coastal Georgia near the Savannah River and later in northeastern Florida.

Yana

The Yana people lived in Northern California on the western slope of the Sierra Nevada Mountains. Their land area was approximately 40 miles long by 60 miles wide and included mountain streams and lush meadows. The people hunted wild game, caught salmon, and gathered roots, acorns, and fruit. Anthropologists estimate that the Yana numbered between 1,500 and 2,000 people. The Yana were divided into four groups: the Northern Yana, the Central Yana, the Southern Yana, and the Yahi, who lived in the southernmost part of the region around the Yuba and Feather rivers. The groups shared a language, but they each had unique dialects and cultural traditions. The Yahi, in particular, were very independent and lived a secluded life. This helped protect them from explorers and settlers into the 19th century. (Source: http://weareca.org/index.php/en/era/precontact/yana_yahi.html)

Yanesha

The Yanesha' or Amuesha people are an ethnic group of the Peruvian Amazon rainforest. The Yanesha' are also known as Amage, Amagues, Amaje, Amajo, Amoishe, Amueixa, Amuese, Amuesha, Amuetamo, Lorenzo, and Omage. The Yanesha people speak the Yanesha', a language belonging to the Maipurean language family, that also includes Asháninka, Yine, and others.

Yanomami

The Yanomami, also spelled Yąnomamö or Yanomama, are a group of indigenous people who live in the Amazon rainforest on the border between Venezuela and Brazil. The Yanomami live in villages usually consisting of their children and extended families. In this largely communal system, the entire village lives under a common roof called the shabono.

Yao

The Yao nationality (its great majority branch is also known as Mien) is a government classification for various minorities in China. They reside in the mountainous terrain of southwest and southern China. They are also an officially recognized ethnic group in Vietnam. There are several distinct groups within the Yao nationality, and they speak several different languages, The Iu Mien make up 70% of the Yao populace.

Yaqui

The Yaqui or Yoeme are Indigenous people whose ancestors originated in the valley of the Río Yaqui in the northern Mexican state of Sonora. Many Yaqui still live in their ancestral homeland. Yaqui speak a dialect of Cahita, a group of about 10 mutually-intelligible languages, most of which are extinct.

Yaquina (Yakonan, Yakon)

Yaquina originally denoted a tribe of Native Americans, now nearly extinct, along with their language, an Alsean language that is also known as Yakwina or Yakona.

Yavapai-Apache

The Yavapai-Apache Nation is comprised of two distinct people, the Yavapai and Apache. The Yavapai refer to themselves as Wipuhk'a'bah and speak the Yuman language, while the Apache refer to themselves as Dil'zhe'e and speak the Athabaskan language. In 1875, our ancestors were forcefully removed from our ancestral homelands in Central Arizona. Today, we continue to reclaim those lands and the culture that was taken from us during the removal. The Yavapai-Apache Nation is located in the Verde Valley and is comprised of five (5) tribal communities: Tunlii, Middle Verde, Rimrock, Camp Verde and Clarkdale. With more than 2,300 enrolled tribal members. (Source: http://yavapai-apache.org/index.htm)

Yazoo

The Yazoo were a tribe of the Native American Tunica people historically located on the lower course of Yazoo River, Mississippi. It was closely connected to other Tunica peoples, especially the Tunica, Koroa, and possibly the Tioux. Nothing is definitely known concerning their language, believed to be related to Tunica, a language isolate.

Yekooche First Nation

The Yekoochet'en (people of Yekooche) have lived in the Stuart Lake area for thousands of years. Situated in a rich area encompassing the Skeena and Fraser watersheds, the community prospered until the arrival of the Europeans. In the beginning, the Yekoochet'en (also known as the Portage Band) shared their resources and knowledge allowing the Hudson's Bay Company. Over the next 150 years the Yekoochet'en saw their rights and way of life consistently eroded as trappers, prospectors and resource companies were given access to their traditional lands. During this time many children were removed from the village at Portage and sent to residential schools where they were prevented from using their own language or practicing their cultural beliefs. Many of the Elders in the community remember those days and share stories of what happened to them when they were cut off from their families.(Source: http://yekooche.com)

Yinka Dene

Yinka Dene is a cover term for the Athabaskan-speaking people of Northern British Columbia. It also serves as the general term for "indigenous person". It literally means "the people on the land". In some dialects, the equivalent Yinka Whut'en is preferred. The people usually known in English as Carrier call themselves Dakelh and prefer to be known by this term. This sounds approximately like da-keth, with the stress on the first syllable. Carrier is a translation of the Sekani name for Dakelh people, Aghele. This term is said to be derived from the fact that when a Dakelh man died and had been cremated, his widow would pack around his bones and ashes during the period of mourning. The reason that the English term comes from the Sekani name is that the first Europeans to enter Dakelh territory, members of the Northwest Company party led by Alexander MacKenzie in 1793, passed through Sekani territory before they entered Dakelh territory and so learned about Dakelh people from the Sekani. Furthermore, Sekani people played an important role in the early period of contact between the fur traders and Dakelh people because some Sekani people could speak both Dakelh and Cree and served as interpreters between the fur traders and Dakelh people. (Source: http://ydli.org/dakinfo/namedak.htm)

Yocot'an (See Tabasco Chontal)

Yoeme (See Yaqui)

Yokaia (Yokaya) (See Pomo)

Yokuts (Yokut, Yokutsan)

The Yokuts (previously known as Mariposans) are a group of Native Americans native to central California. Prior to European contact, the Yokuts consisted of up to 60 separate Tribes speaking the same language. "Yokuts" means "People." Conventional sub-groupings include the Foothill Yokuts, Northern Valley Yokuts, and Southern Valley Yokuts.

Yolngu

The Yolngu or Yolŋu are an Indigenous Australian people inhabiting northeastern Arnhem Land in the Northern Territory of Australia. Yolngu means "person" in the Yolŋu languages. Yolngu speak a dozen dialects of a language group known as Yolngu Matha.

Ysleta del Sur (Also see Tiwa)

The Ysleta del Sur Pueblo ("the Pueblo") is a U.S. federally recognized Native American tribe and sovereign nation. The Pueblo is one of three tribes located in Texas and the only Pueblo located in the state. The Tribal community, known as "Tigua", was established in 1682 after the Pueblo Revolt of 1680. Since then, the Tribe has retained a significant presence in the El Paso region that helped pave the way for the development of the area. The Tribe maintains its traditional political system and ceremonial practices and continues to flourish as a Pueblo community. Tribal enrolment is over 1,600 citizens. (Source: http://ysletadelsurpueblo.org/)

Yucatec Maya (Yucateco, Yucatan)

Yucatec Maya, called Màaya t'àan (lit. "Maya speech") by its speakers, is a Mayan language spoken in the Yucatán Peninsula and northern Belize. To native speakers, it is known only as Maya – "Yucatec" is a tag linguists use to distinguish it from other Mayan languages (such as K'iche' and Itza' Maya).

Yuchi (Yuchee)

The Yuchi, also spelled Euchee and Uchee, are a Native American Tribe who traditionally lived in the eastern Tennessee River valley in Tennessee in the 16th century. Today the Yuchi live primarily in the northeastern Oklahoma area, where many are enrolled as citizens in the federally recognized Muscogee Creek Nation. Yuchi is commonly interpreted to mean "over there sit/live" or "situated yonder." Their autonym is Coyaha or Tsoyaha, meaning "Children of the Sun."

Yuin

Yuin people (aka Thurga) are those Australian Aborigines from the South Coast of New South Wales. All Yuin people share ancestors who spoke one or more of the Yuin language dialects, including Djiringanj, Thaua, Walbanga, or Wandandian.

Yuki (Yukian)

The Yuki are an indigenous people of California, whose traditional territory is around Round Valley, Mendocino County. The Yuki call themselves the autonym Ukomno'm, meaning "Valley People."

Yuma (See Quechan)

Yupik (Yup'ik, Yuit)

The Yupik are a group of indigenous or Aboriginal peoples of western, southwestern, and southcentral Alaska and the Russian Far East. They are related to the Inuit and Iñupiat peoples. Yup'ik (plural Yupiit) comes from the Yup'ik word yuk meaning "person" plus the post-base -pik meaning "real" or "genuine." Thus, it means literally "real people."

Yurok (Yu'rok)

The Yurok, whose name means "downriver people" in the neighbouring Karuk language, are Native Americans who live in northwestern California near the Klamath River and Pacific coast. Their autonym is Olekwo'l meaning "Persons." Yurok is one of two Algic languages spoken in California, the other being Wiyot.

Zapotec

The Zapotecs are an indigenous people of Mexico. The population is concentrated in the southern state of Oaxaca, There are four basic groups of Zapotecs: the istmeños, the serranos, the southern Zapotecs, and the Central Valley Zapotecs. The name Zapotec is an exonym coming from Nahuatl tzapotēcah , which means "inhabitants of the place of sapote." The Zapotecs call themselves Be'ena'a, which means "The People."

Zia

The Zia are an indigenous tribe centered at Zia Pueblo, an Indian reservation in New Mexico. The Zia are known for their pottery and use of the Sun symbol. The people are a branch of the large Pueblo community.

Zimshian (See Tsimshian)

Zoque

The Zoque are an indigenous people of Mexico; they speak variants of the Zoque languages. They live mainly in the northerly sector of Chiapas state but also in the state of Oaxaca. Their language is also called Zoque, and has several branches and dialects. The Zoque are related to the Mixe. They follow the Roman Catholic religion.

Zuma (Zumana) (See Suma)

Zuni

The ancient homelands of the Zunis are along the middle reaches of the Zuni River where their cultural ancestors lived for centuries. Near the settlements and villages

left by the ancient people, the Zuni Indians built compact villages of multi-storied houses. These were the towns seen and lived by Coronado and his men and called them the "Seven Cities" in the land of Cibola. The mythical Seven Cities of Cibola (Spanish word for "buffalo") lured Coronado to the southwest in 1540 in a treasure quest. Unfortunately, with the exception of the village of Zuni, all those sites were abandoned long ago. For the last three hundred years, most of the Indians had lived in a single village, the Pueblo of Zuni. Within the boundaries often small, rather cramped reservation are smaller farming villages at Pescado, Nutria, and Ojo Caliente, which were established probably in the eighteenth century but which in more recent years have been occupied only during the time of planting and harvest. Beyond the boundaries of the reservation, there are ancient sites and areas, sacred points and shrines, and places of pilgrimage central to Zuni life and history. (Source: http://ashiwi.org/History.aspx)

Nancy Shanawdithit

Nancy Shanawdithit was the last known living member of the Beothuk people of Newfoundland, Canada
Born: 1801 Died: June 6, 1829, St. John's, Newfoundland.